Jim tells it straight up. *God Is Still Talking* will challenge your complacency, sharpen your understanding, and encourage your journey.

—Paul S. Williams
President, The Orchard Group

God Still Speaks is a passionate plea for his readers to be sensitive and alert to the many ways God guides and directs. He is careful to harmonize and subordinate more subjective avenues of God's guidance to the revealed Word of God, while he calls for dedicated effort to expand one's spiritual listening resources.

—Dr. David Eubanks
President Emeritus, Johnson Bible College

# GOD IS STILL TALKING

Dr. James E. Hamer

*James E. Hamer*

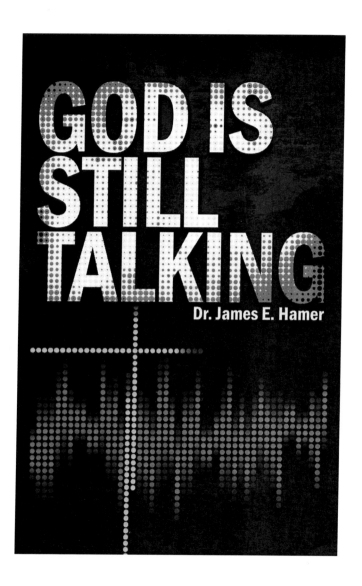

# GOD IS STILL TALKING

**Dr. James E. Hamer**

TATE PUBLISHING & *Enterprises*

Published by Tate Publishing & Enterprises, LLC
127 E. Trade Center Terrace | Mustang, Oklahoma 73064 USA
1.888.361.9473 | www.tatepublishing.com

Tate Publishing is committed to excellence in the publishing industry. The company reflects the philosophy established by the founders, based on Psalm 68:11,
*"The Lord gave the word and great was the company of those who published it."*

Book design copyright © 2009 by Tate Publishing, LLC. All rights reserved.
*Cover design by Joshua Hamer & Tyler Evans*
*Interior design by Jeff Fisher*

Published in the United States of America

ISBN: 978-1-60799-497-8
1. Religion, Spirituality
2. Religion, Christian Life, Devotional
09.06.05

# DEDICATION

This book is dedicated to Kathleen G. Hamer (March 28, 1915–September 26, 2008) who was one extraordinary woman that loved her family and believed in me. This dedication is in praise for her unshakeable faith in the Lord, her belief in the power of the church, and her tireless service to Jesus. She was one of the most positive people I have ever met, who knew no obstacle that could not be overcome. This book fulfills a promise to her that I would write a book and have it published. She didn't live to see the fulfillment of her confidence. However, I have a suspicion that even as I write this dedication, she knows and is aware of this process. Thank you, Mom, for your love and prayers and confidence in me.

# ACKNOWLEDGEMENTS

This book would not have been written without the encouragement and the persistence of my wife and children. They pressed me to complete what I started and what I doubted was valuable for the kingdom. Bonnie, my wife, and Joshua, Janelle, and Jennifer, my children—all of them served as readers of the manuscript, offering their critical insights and their assurance that the material was truly interesting. I also thank their spouses, Lynn, Jose, and Nate, for their support and belief in me. In addition, God blessed all of us with my first grandchild, Aubree Noel Hamer, who found her way two times in this book. My family is a treasure from God.

I want to especially recognize Elizabeth Nevel, my mother-in-law, for the difficult task of editing much of the material. She found so many grammar errors, misspellings, and illogical sentences that she deserves the credit for saving the editors of this manuscript even more hours of time. Elizabeth is an avid reader. She knows good books and good reading. And she is pretty good at Scrabble.

Lastly, I want to acknowledge my church family, East Northport Christian Church, that gives me constant response to my preaching and teaching. These wonderful people can be found in the pages of this book. I want them to know how I value their support and their challenges to our ministry together. They are a means through which God is still talking to me.

# TABLE OF CONTENTS

# FOREWORD

"I've been meaning to write this email to you for a while now. It's an experience that I had recently that showed me God's truly amazing power and wisdom … I felt drained by all these experiences. I saw God work so many times and I felt so close to Him." "I was reminded this week of how God equips us with His Word. (After reading Matthew 3) The very next day at a dental appointment, my dentist said to me, 'Okay … well what about baptism? There's a lot of differing opinions out there …' Wow–God's hand was in this! I had just studied it the night before. I quoted some Scripture to him…" "I was cracked up this morning when your sermon started and you talked about Amazing Jesus. We had the most beautiful sunrise this morning … I turned to Delaney and said (I'm not kidding!), 'Isn't God amazing, baby? Look at the sunrise He's given us.' So I guess my brain was already tuned into the message before I even arrived." "What transpired that Sunday was all about being still and knowing my God. If you remember, you and I talked about prayer and discussing what to pray and how much and how long, etc. I shared with you that I was in the prayer room all prayed out and God spoke through the silence and said 'Be still and know that I am God.' As close as I can determine it was at that time God carried my son to be with him."

God is still talking. These email fragments from several people in my network attest to the premise of this book. I have hundreds of them on file. They are a constant reminder of the lessons to be learned from this book. Jim Hamer has written a highly practical and Biblically sound presentation of how God speaks to us and how we can learn to hear him more effectively. As Jim states, "God is still talking." The real question is: "Are You Listening?"

Jim writes from the deep well of many years of ministry. He draws from hundreds of experiences where God has made Himself known. Jim is a highly educated person, yet his training has not left him with eyes that cannot see, and ears that cannot hear God's activity in daily life. He knows God still speaks. He has witnessed it many times.

While theologians and seminary professors formalize and debate the issue, thousands of common, every day Christians hear and witness God's communication regularly. Jim's book will help you to be one of those people who hear God's voice as part of your daily existence. He explains how God uses numerous avenues to make Himself known. Jim will teach you how to listen.

Take your time with this book. Savor its' lessons. Implement a principle or an idea, then return to the book for the next adventure. God is still speaking. "He who has ears, let him hear."

—Dr. Don M. Hamilton
Senior Pastor, Capital Area Christian Church

# INTRODUCTION

God is still talking. Maybe that doesn't surprise all Christians, or all people for that matter. But for many Christians, that statement can cause much study, discussion, disagreement, and ultimately, confusion. Generally, the question asked is: Does God still speak today? This question arises from some theological conclusion that God has spoken to us in his Word, that the sum and substance of what God wants to say to us has been written. So if one desires to know what God is saying, one must give intense attention to studying and meditating on the Bible.

This book makes the question a statement. God *is* still talking. The real question is: Are you listening? And the question seriously confronts you as the reader. If you are a Christian, it challenges you as one who has access to Jesus as much as any preacher or any self-proclaimed spokesperson of God. God is talking to you. It is more likely that you are just unaware that he is speaking to you, that he is leading you, that he is teaching you, that he is pointing to spiritual lessons that constantly surround you.

This book seeks to help everyone perk up their ears and to hear God talking. For, after all, the more of us who are listening and who are speaking to one another the things we are hearing, the greater will be our ability to discern what God is saying and doing and directing us to do.

# Breakthrough: The Monday Power Word

In recent years, I began e-mailing to my church family, friends, relatives, and acquaintances the Monday Power Word. I heard about this idea some years back, but I don't know whom to give the credit. I hesitated to engage this discipline for some time. However, something or someone kept this before my mind until I just had to plunge into it.

Ministers have plenty to do, believe it or not. With the necessary work of preparing a well-written, well-delivered sermon every week, weekly Bible studies, prayers for every occasion, funeral messages, weddings, and the list goes on, I did not relish the thought of writing anything more. So I began doing it with some fear that I would run out of material and that I would have nothing to say. I think about that now and say to myself, what a stupid thought.

The Monday Power Word is not just a word, but a Monday morning thought. It is intended to give a boost to everyone who needs to get the engine running on Monday mornings. I stay committed to that goal every week (well, okay, it doesn't always get done). There is pressure to ensure that the word is simple, short, and encouraging.

In the beginning, the Monday Power Word was mostly driven by a single verse of Scripture. Every Monday, the main task involved finding the encouraging Scripture to carry people through the coming week. But along the way I began recognizing that not all of those short e-mails were being driven by

Scripture as the starting point. I began noting ideas for future power words. And the source for some of those thoughts became strange for me (birds, waves, garbage dumps).

I still feel pressure writing every Monday morning. But there is an expectation now. Depending on the word for the day, various people take the time to respond and add their appreciation or insight to what was written. That encourages me. And a good number have recommended that these Monday Power Words be put into book form. Wow! I have never really regarded them as carrying that much impact!

But I try to listen, not just to the wonderful people who surround me, but to God. I didn't get a great sense from him that fifty-two Monday Power Words were really what this was all about. I came to the conclusion that it is really about God, and the fact that he is still talking.

I can't produce fifty-two Power Words a year that are really excellent (and not all of them are). I would have run out of material a long time ago had I not become aware that God is still talking, all the time and in many ways. When I look back on some of them, I am amazed that any of those thoughts came from me. And when I consider how some of them came to be, I know that God was communicating those thoughts, insights, and ideas.

This book is really about all of us. God hasn't just chosen to speak to me. I believe that he is always talking to every one of us. Most of us simply are not aware. The Monday Power Word helped me to become aware. I will share throughout this book various Power Words and illustrations of how they came to be. I hope that it will help everyone's ears listen to what God is saying to all of us throughout the day. For God is still talking!

## Some Theological Caution

There are a great many Christians who state something similar to the following: "God spoke to me about..." Many of us get a little uneasy with those statements, especially when some "revelations" seem to run counter to what God has already spoken. Nothing in the introduction or in any part of this book should be misconstrued as giving license or credibility to that communication. This can account for some of the hesitation to accept that God is still talking today.

A Christian who is hearing something directly from God that offers some teaching or direction contrary to the Scripture is being deceived. God does not speak something that contradicts his confirmed and sealed word. He does not give us the license to make some decision that conflicts with his stated will. For example, can we rationalize being defiant to the assignments of our boss? Provided that those tasks do not lead us to sin and to oppose God, we should "serve wholeheartedly, as if you were serving the Lord, not people" (Ephesians 6:7) There is no rationalization for anything less.

I get uncomfortable with Christians who are hearing directly from God but seem to have no understanding or regard for the Scripture. They are living apart from the foundation. Hearing God speak requires a sure foundation that does not change. John warned his readers about following false spirits. He gave this direction as a foundation for determining what is true or false:

> As for you, see that what you have heard from the beginning remains in you. If it does, you also will remain in the Son and in the Father. And this is what he promised us—eternal life. I am writing these things to you about those who are trying to lead you astray. As for you, the anointing you received from him remains in you, and you do not need anyone to teach you. But as his anointing teaches you about all things and as that anointing is real, not counterfeit—just as it has taught you, remain in him.
>
> 1 John 2:24–27

The Scripture serves as the beginning foundation for hearing God speak. It contains "the faith that the Lord has once for all entrusted to us, his people." (Jude 3) All of the ways that God is still talking are subject to his sure word.

On the other side, there are Christians whose relationship to God seems to be more a relationship to Scripture. In our approach to Scripture and to life, we send a message that God spoke in the record of the Bible and that there is nothing more to be said. We wrestle with Scriptures such as "For those who are led by the Spirit of God are the children of God" and "The Spirit testifies with our spirit that we are children of God" (Romans 8:14, 16). How does the Spirit testify with our spirit? How are we led by the Spirit? We struggle to explain that teaching and to display it freely in our lives. We move forward cautiously, wondering if we have God's guidance in matters not specifically addressed in the Bible.

We must find the balance between what God has spoken and what he is continuing to say, with the Bible in the center of the whole conversation. All Christians need to see the Bible as more dynamic, living, and fresh. Consider what the Scripture teaches about itself.

> "For the word of God is *alive and active*. Sharper than any double-edged sword, it penetrates even to dividing soul and spirit, joints and marrow; it judges the thoughts and attitudes of the heart. Nothing in all creation is hidden from God's sight. Everything is uncovered and laid bare before the eyes of him to whom we must give an account.
>
> Hebrews 4:12, 13

Alive, active, penetrating, judging—sounds pretty dynamic to me. But there are questions about the word. When we want guidance and help, how do we experience it as "living and active"? When we are uncertain, how do we tap its "penetrating" power? These questions alongside these verses require some further discussion in another chapter.

It is important for us to see how the Scripture directed the affairs of the church in the first century. Notice how the early church referred to Scripture in a prayer that asked God for the boldness to speak:

You spoke by the Holy Spirit through the mouth of your servant, our father David: "Why do the nations rage and the people plot in vain? The kings of the earth rise up and the rulers band together against the Lord and against his anointed one."

Acts 4:25, 26

Note all the elements at work here. There is the Holy Spirit speaking through David, who wrote down a communication that was still applicable to the situation facing the new community of Christians in Jerusalem. This account in Scripture provides a great example of how the Word of God remains relevant throughout the ages.

Scripture is always at work in all the ways that God is still talking to us today. People who want to hear clearly from God must have a solid foundation in understanding the Bible. The words of Scripture are no less the words of the Holy Spirit than any direct words that we are hearing today that are true.

And so, even as the thesis is posed that God is still talking, it is important that we first lay a theological foundation for that proposition.

This book is divided into two parts. The first part lays the foundation for the possibility that God is still talking in many times and in many ways. The second part explores some of those ways that God awakens us and directs us. Some Monday Power Words are given as examples generated from hearing him speak in various ways.

# Part One

## Chapter 1

# GOD SPOKE

God spoke. Those two words sum up completely what separates Christian faith and the Christian worldview from every other religion and every other philosophy. We live in the confidence that God spoke. As Francis Schaeffer states in one of his books, "He is there and he is not silent."

The Creator of the universe, the One who gives life and breath to all things, reached out to us. There was no demand that he do it. There was no need in himself to do it. It is simply a part of his nature and his grace. He wanted us to know him. He wanted us to know ourselves. He wanted us to understand life. He didn't set us on this planet, floating through space, without a roadmap to find our way.

Apart from him, we don't know anything with any confidence. Those who choose to live without any regard for him can be seen drifting through life. The New Testament designates those people as "lost." But even with people who disregard the Creator, he continues to reach out. "For the Son of Man came to seek and to save what was lost" (Luke 19:10).

God is tirelessly trying to speak to people. We are created in his image, set apart from all the rest of creation, for that very purpose. The Bible remains forever as a testimony to God extending himself to people and his creation. He just doesn't stop. It is not a matter that God is not talking. It is always a matter that we harden our hearts so as not to hear. We simply need to be more discerning of all the ways he uses to reach our ears.

## God Spoke

The Hebrew writer states that God spoke. He sets this forth in a definitive and unquestionable manner in the prologue of his writing. It is meant to fix any doubt about this in the minds of the readers. He writes:

> In the past God spoke to our ancestors through the prophets at many times and in various ways, but in these last days he has spoken to us by his Son, whom he appointed heir of all things, and through whom also he made the universe.
>
> Hebrews 1:1, 2

It is important for us to explore this Scripture in more detail with regard to its impact upon the thesis that God is still talking. Does this Scripture teach that God has spoken finally and forever and is never speaking again? Has God said everything that he intends to say, and are we to figure out everything from his written record? Does this Scripture put an end to God talking?

The Christians who were receiving this letter were Hebrew in descent. They were people who believed the Old Testament Scriptures. They trusted the prophets and the record of the Scripture they possessed. They had no doubt about the fact that God spoke in the past through the prophets.

What is new is the truth that God spoke through the Son—through Jesus. These Hebrew Christians were drifting away from their faith and confidence in Jesus. The letter to the Hebrews exalts the person and the work of Jesus Christ. The writer presents him as superior to the prophets, the angels, Moses, the high priest, and Melchizedek. He is the mediator of a new covenant about which the prophets wrote. Thus, it is critical that the Hebrews, as well as we today, keep our eyes fixed on him with an enduring faith like the heroes of faith in the past. This summarizes the main message and contents of the letter.

The writer wants to establish with the Hebrew Christians that as surely as God spoke in the past through the prophets, he spoke just as firmly by Jesus in these last days. In both cases, the word "spoke" indicates the idea of something that is established. He spoke. It is something that is done and unalterable. There is a sense of finality to the action that is described.

The writer expands on this later in the letter. After presenting Jesus as superior to the angels, and having already stated that God spoke in Jesus, he urges the readers to "pay the most careful attention" to what they heard. They already knew that the message spoken by angels was firm. How much more, then, is the word of salvation spoken through Jesus?

This salvation, which was first announced by the Lord, was confirmed to us by those who heard him. God also testified to it by signs, wonders and various miracles, and by gifts of the Holy Spirit distributed according to his will.

Hebrews 2: 3, 4

The focus of this teaching centers on the reliability of the message that was spoken, whether by the prophets, the angels, or the Son. It is a word that is unalterable, confirmed, and sure. These words express the idea of the same word in the original language. In the New International Version of the Bible, verse two is translated as "for since the message spoken through angels *was binding*" (*bebaios*). The New American Standard version translates that same word as "*proven unalterable.*" However, the same word in the original language is translated as "*was confirmed*" (*bebaios*) in verse three of the above verses. The writer clearly wants us to understand that the word that the angels spoke, the word that the Son spoke, and the word that those who heard Jesus speak was firm or sure or unalterable.

We find this same word in Peter's second letter with regard to the prophetic message. Peter reflects back on the time when he and John were with Jesus on the mountain when God spoke: "This is my Son, whom I love; with him I am well pleased" (2 Peter 1:17). This gave him even more confidence that Jesus was the Christ. And it gave added confidence to the prophetic word. Peter writes: "We also have the prophetic message as something completely reliable (*bebaios*), and you will do well to pay attention to it, as to a light shining in a dark place, until the day dawns and the morning star rises in your hearts" (2 Peter 1:19).

The major thrust in all of the above exhortations seeks to awaken the attention of the readers to this word that God spoke, whether it is the Old Testament or the Scripture being written in their own time. That message is reliable, verified, sure, and unalterable—whatever word one wishes to use. It is useful to apply all of them in order to be absolutely clear that God spoke, and what he has spoken is done and will not change.

## God's Written Word Speaks

Christians understand that God still speaks through Scripture. "All Scripture is God-breathed and is *useful* for teaching, rebuking, correcting and training in righteousness so that all God's people may be thoroughly equipped for every good work (2 Timothy 3:16, 17). It can't be said more clearly. The Scripture "equips" us "thoroughly."

This gives insight to Paul's admonition to Timothy. "Do your best to present yourself to God as one approved, a worker who does not need to be ashamed and who correctly handles the word of truth" (2 Timothy 2:15). Being raised in the church and regularly attending Bible school, I still like the version of this verse which all of us memorized: "Study to shew yourself approved as a workman who does not need to be ashamed, rightly dividing the word of truth" ("KJV"). Timothy was confronting the problem of false teaching involving "myths and endless genealogies" (1

Timothy 1:3, 4). Understanding God's direction for our life and ministry, discerning truth from error, and hearing God and not the Deceiver, requires careful, serious Bible study. It is the starting point for all that God is speaking.

We see this at work early in the book of Acts. Peter explains to the believers gathered around him that Judas must be replaced. He cites Scripture that was written hundreds of years ago as the reason for this action. He states, "Brothers and sisters, the Scripture had to be fulfilled in which the Holy Spirit spoke long ago through David concerning Judas, who served as a guide for those who arrested Jesus" (Acts 1:16). God was continuing to direct the current ministry of the disciples through Scripture. He is still the head of his church today and desires to direct our affairs. But it requires that we handle it rightly so that we don't use what is written as a proof text for something we want to believe or something we want to do that is contrary to his clear will, law, or purpose.

Paul states clearly the relationship of Scripture to our present circumstances. He wrote to the Roman Christians:

> For everything written in the past was written to teach us, so that through the endurance taught in the Scriptures and the encouragement they provide we might have hope. May the God who gives endurance and encouragement give you the same attitude of mind toward each other that Christ Jesus had, so that with one mind and one voice we may glorify the God and Father of our Lord Jesus Christ.
>
> Romans 15:4, 5

Scripture serves to teach us. It teaches us endurance and provides encouragement. However, notice that Paul says God gives endurance and encouragement. So who or what gives endurance and encouragement? Is it Scripture or is it God? Both Scripture and God work toward the same results. These two Scriptures are almost parallel statements with verse 5 defining verse 4. Both God and the Scripture seek the same objective in these verses. The ultimate goal is that the Romans might, in their present circumstance, have one mind and one voice in glorifying God. The Scripture and God want to affect the present circumstance. That makes this a "living and active" word. For the Scripture *speaks*—present tense. And it is none other than God speaking.

## What Is Different?

Having examined all of this, we must note that the Hebrew writer presents a contrast concerning the fact that God has spoken. This contrast is critical to the thesis of this book. What are the particulars in this contrast?

The writer makes a distinction between the past and the last days. The emphasis in these verses is on this difference. The Bible draws a line in history between two epochs. There is a period of history when God spoke in many ways and at different times. God chose different modes to communicate his message, i.e., dreams, visions, a small voice, etc. He spoke at different times through various people. The opening verse of Hebrews is not meant to limit this communication to just the prophets. In this letter, he spoke through angels, and he spoke through Moses. It includes all the people who received God's message and proclaimed it to the people in the past.

We refer to the past revelation as being progressive. While the prophets proclaimed many truths to their contemporary circumstance, contained within their prophecies was a message concerning the last days. It was a message specifically about the coming salvation of God. Peter explains, "Concerning this salvation, the prophets, who spoke of the grace that was to come to you, searched intently and with the greatest care, trying to find out the time and circumstances to which the Spirit of Christ in them was pointing when he predicted the sufferings of Christ and the glories that would follow" (1 Peter 1:10, 11).

With the coming of Jesus, a new epoch dawned, referred to as the last days. It was the current time of the Hebrew Christians, and it is still our current time now in Bible history. We live in the epoch of the last days. While it required a number of different people over the course of time in the first epoch to speak about this salvation, in these last days God spoke through his Son. It is a contrast between the past and now, between many and one, and most importantly, between a salvation future and a salvation complete.

Various commentators apply phrases such as "God's final word" or "God's once for all word" to the above contrast. The sense of these conclusions raises the question of what exactly is meant by these phrases? Do they infer that God spoke and that there is nothing more for him to say? Does he no longer speak in dreams or visions or through a still small voice to us, his children? Does the contrast drawn in the opening verses of Hebrews consist in the elimination of these modes of speaking? To what does God's final word refer? Reading most commentators, one draws a conclusion that God has spoken finally and completely, and he has nothing more to say.

So, has God spoken finally or is he still talking? The answer is yes. Yes, he has spoken unalterably in Jesus. But he has also spoken unalterably through the prophets. While the Hebrew writer drew a contrast, there is still continuity in God speaking. Through the Old Testament prophets, God spoke unalterably about his purposes, plans, and promises. The message spoken through Moses was the law of God that could not be changed. The message spoken through angels was binding. All of the communication pointed to the Son and the salvation to come.

There is a message spoken through Jesus that is final, that is the culmination of all that God spoke throughout Old Testament. It concerns the salvation established in the Son, and it is finished, done, unchangeable. It is the final word on the redemption that God began in the garden and concluded in the death, burial, and resurrection of Jesus. There is nothing more to be said with regard to "so great a salvation."

This record of God's completed activity, prophesied in the Old Testament and fulfilled in the redemptive work of Jesus, places us in a new era of time. That's the true contrast presented in the opening verses of Hebrews. The contrast is not between speaking in various ways in one era and now, in this new era, having spoken through Jesus with nothing more to say. It is a contrast between two eras of time. Far from retreating into silence, God places all of us in a far more active dimension of communication. There is more noise and more people involved. I submit that he is still talking, for it is an active and living word plus more.

# Chapter 2

# LET'S TAKE THE LID OFF

Something dramatically changed after the resurrection and ascension of Christ. The world took on a whole new perspective from anything people previously experienced. It is not that the universe changed, but that we were given new access to this greater dimension of living. We became aware of something more real. We are taught to live in the fuller reality of this universe that consists of "things in heaven and on earth, visible and invisible, whether thrones or powers or rulers or authorities" (Colossians 1:16).

Now, it is not that people did not have some concept of the existence of something more than the ordinary things of life. The world has always had its gods. "Paul then stood up in the meeting of the Areopagus and said: 'People of Athens! I see that in every way you are very religious. For as I walked around and looked carefully at your objects of worship, I even found an altar with this inscription: To An Unknown God" (Acts 17:22, 23). And there was plenty of discussion about these matters. "All the Athenians and the foreigners who lived there spent their time doing nothing but talking about and listening to the latest ideas" (Acts 17:21).

And it just wasn't the religiously minded that

engaged in thinking about something other than this existence. Socrates, Plato, Aristotle, and more discussed the other dimension of life. We still refer to the wisdom of the ancient Greeks to this day.

All of this amounted to speculation—thoughts, hopes, dreams, and words on paper without true or real substance. For those more religiously minded, it really was one-dimensional. It consisted of reaching out to some god out there without any expectation of a response.

To sum it up, there was and still is a lot of talk, a lot of words, a lot of philosophizing, but little life. I call them dead words. They simply get swallowed up by the limits of what we can know about life apart from God. In contrast, our Scriptures state that what we possess in writing is "alive and active and sharper than any two-edged sword" (Hebrews 4:12). How can that be? What makes the words of Scripture "alive?"

## A Different, Fearsome Jesus

It's remarkable if you haven't read it for a while. Take the time and read the vision of John that he saw concerning Jesus (Revelation 1:9–20). The imagery takes you back to the vision of Daniel as recorded in Daniel 7:8–14. I must resist the urge to divert and fill in some of the drama set forth from both Daniel and John. It is a story that centers in Jesus, the Son of Man, fearsome and reigning with eternal power!

For our purposes here, specifically note this part of the description John gives about Jesus: "In his right hand he held seven stars, and coming out of his mouth was a *sharp, double-edged sword*" (Revelation 1:16). I can't cite any commentator who understands this sword to refer to anything else but the word of God. It is Jesus' weapon of conquest and victory.

Later in Revelation, John provides another picture of Jesus:

> I saw heaven standing open and there before me was a white horse, whose rider is called Faithful and True. With justice he judges and makes war. His eyes are like blazing fire, and on his head are many crowns. He has a name written on him that no one knows but he himself. He is dressed in a robe dipped in blood, and his name is the Word (logos) of God. The armies of heaven were following him, riding on white horses and dressed in fine linen, white and clean. Coming out of his mouth is a sharp sword with which to strike down the nations.
>
> Revelation 19:11–15

What an awesome picture of Jesus! This is quite different than the one described in the gospels or even of the picture presented of him after his resurrection where he was mistaken for a gardener or when he made breakfast for his disciples by the Sea of Galilee. This picture in Revelation is wonderful, fearsome, striking, and now!

One of the hardest mental blocks for people to overcome with regard to Revelation is the concept that it deals with matters that are future. Most people are comfortable with the first three chapters of the letter, but when people and commentators get to chapter four and beyond, it gets a little crazy. So many commentators put those chapters in some future setting.

Jesus commissioned John to write: "Write, therefore what you have seen, both *what is now* and what will take place later" (Revelation 1:19). What are the things that are now? Let's see if we can put the story together.

First, John's experience was a now reality. We may get tripped up by commentators and by our bibles when both describe Revelation 1:9–20 as John's vision of Christ. It is a vision in the sense that John describes Jesus in vivid symbols. But make no mistake about it; this is Jesus whom John is encountering in a concrete manner. It happens at a real place, the island of Patmos. It happens on a real day, the Lord's Day. He hears real speech, the voice of Jesus who gave John clear instructions. This is not too very different than what he experienced when Jesus took John, James, and Peter to a mountain and was transfigured before them. Jesus simply peeled back the veil of the invisible and allowed John to see what was present around him at that very moment.

Second, we might want to inquire what is meant by John's own self-awareness that he "was in the Spirit." Note how a couple of commentators regard this statement: That is, he was projected forward in his inner self in a vision, not bodily, to the future day of the Lord when God will pour out His judgments on the earth.

Jamieson, Fausset, and Brown comment that he was:

> In a state of ecstasy; the outer world being shut out, and the inner and higher life or spirit being taken full possession of by God's Spirit, so that an immediate connection with the invisible world is established. While the prophet "speaks" in the Spirit, the apocalyptic seer is in the Spirit in his whole person. The spirit only (that which connects us with God and the invisible world) is active, or rather recipient, in the apocalyptic state. With Christ this being "in the Spirit" was not the exception, but his continual state.[1]

Some other commentators describe John as being in "charismatic worship" or "in a visionary state." All of these descriptions place John in some state other than one's normal living. Thus, being "in the Spirit" requires reaching some state of being other than what's common in our daily life. This understanding takes John's experience and our experience totally out of the realm of our daily life.

This contradicts Paul's teaching about life in the Spirit. He writes: "You, however, are not controlled by the sinful nature but are in the Spirit, if indeed the Spirit of God lives in you" (Romans 8:9). Just as being "in the Spirit" is Christ's continual state, so it is with us. If we are aware and mindful of our new life in Christ, we are always in the Spirit. We have daily, continual, moment-by-moment access to God through Jesus. We simply need to remind ourselves of this relationship. The fact that it happened on the Lord's Day is not critical for understanding. John simply identified the day of the week that he had this unusual encounter with Jesus. It could have happened on any day that we are "in the Spirit." Isn't that the true realm of our life every day, every moment?

Third, we must see the activity taking place in this vision. After hearing the voice behind him, John turned around and described this: "I saw seven golden lamp stands, and among the lamp stands was someone like a son of man, dressed in a robe reaching down to his feet and with a golden sash around his chest" (Revelation 1:12, 13). We know that the lamp stands were the seven churches to whom this letter was being sent out (Revelation 1:20). Thus we have, at that very moment in time, Jesus moving in the midst of those seven churches.

All of the above from Revelation was a now reality. Applying this to ourselves, we might say that wherever we are at this moment, we are in the Spirit, and Jesus is present in our midst. He is present in a wonderful, fearsome, and dynamic way. He moves about us and about the nations as the glorified, exalted, faithful and true, judge and king. "The kingdom of the world has become the kingdom of our Lord and his Messiah, and he will reign forever and ever" (Revelation 11:15). And "coming out of his mouth is a sharp sword with which to strike down the nations… He treads (is treading) the winepress of the fury of the wrath of God Almighty" (Revelation 19:15).

We live in a far more active universe than what we tend to recognize in our mundane living. Jesus is on the move in judgment and conquest. Nothing more is needed to win the victory than the weapon of his word.

## The Word: He/It's Dynamic

In a recent Bible study, in the midst of some discussion about spiritual things, someone made the observation that many people don't see studying the Bible as having the same level of spirituality as people who are engaged in charismatic worship. I would guess that a great host of people would share that observation, including people who regularly engage in Bible study. We have made it more an academic exercise than a matter of spiritual living. Yet, we are presented with the truth that the word is far more energetic.

"For the word (logos) of God [is] living and active (energetic) and sharper than any two edged sword" (Hebrews 4:12). The living word has the capacity for vigorous activity. It contains available power for the accomplishment of what it was designed to achieve. How can something like that be boring and dry and spiritually deficient? Maybe it is because he can't get a word in edgewise!

There is much commentary discussion about the word of God in this verse. Is this a reference to the Scripture or does it refer to Jesus, the Logos? Nearly everybody comes to the conclusion that it refers to Scripture or to the proclamation of the Scripture (Hebrews 4:2). It is interesting how the subject of discussion changes in verse 13 of that section. We have just been told that this word of God "penetrates even to dividing soul and spirit, joints and marrow; it judges the thoughts and attitudes of the heart." Notice how the subject changes in the next verse. "Nothing in all creation is hidden from *God's* sight. Everything is uncovered and laid bare before the eyes of him to whom we must give account" (Hebrews 4:13).

So which is it that judges and uncovers the thoughts and attitudes of the heart? To what must we give an account? Is it the Scripture or God?

It is no accident that Revelation gives us both the word of God as the weapon proceeding out of the mouth of Jesus and also the conquering Jesus as the Word of God. We must always see them together. The One who is alive, who is reigning, gives life to the words of Scripture. Maybe we could liken this operation to that of a Walt Disney cartoonist who draws the images of his characters on paper, but through the process of animation lifts them off the pages. We experience those characters as alive—dancing, singing, talking, conquering, and drawing us into their world. Can you see the master artist Jesus making the words come alive? They are no longer simply marks inscribed on paper, but a world to be experienced and lived! They are words that are talking! It is God, judging, uncovering, and laying bare our lives so that something more perfect might take shape.

## Alive in Proclamation

The familiar Scripture about the word of God arises in the real life situation of these Christians. They were slipping away from their faith and conviction in Jesus. The Hebrew writer presents to them the superiority of Jesus with the objective that they would "hold firmly to our confidence and the hope in which we glory" (Hebrews 3:6).

It is instructive to recall how these Christians believed in Jesus in the first place. They responded to a message that they heard. "We must pay the most careful attention, therefore, to what we have heard, so that we do not drift away" (Hebrews 2:1). And in the same chapter in which we find the familiar Scripture concerning the activity of the word of God, we read just before those verses: "For we also have had the good news proclaimed to us, just as they did; but the message they heard was of no value to them, because they did not share the faith of those who obeyed" (Hebrews 4:2). Both of these verses introduce us into a dynamic context of the proclamation of the good news, the message of salvation.

These Christians to whom the writer sends this letter are Israelites. They are becoming like their ancestors who also went astray from the ways of God. So he takes them back to that time when the Israelites tested and rebelled against God in the wilderness. They too had the word of God proclaimed to them. They hardened their hearts and failed to enter into the promised land. The Hebrew writer admonishes them not follow to the example of the ancestors.

What is instructive is how the proclamation of the word is linked to the presence of God. The Israelites in the wilderness had the word proclaimed to them, but the Hebrew writer says they were turning "away from the living God" (Hebrews 3:12). Moses presented God's instructions to the people, but the Scripture says in Psalm 95, and the Hebrew writer notes, that they were hardening their hearts to the voice of God. Three times in Hebrews the writer references Psalm 95:7: "Today, if you hear *his voice,* do not harden your hearts" (Hebrews 3:7, 15, 4:7). It was God speaking through the mouth of Moses. It is still God speaking through the writings of Moses. And wherever the good news is being proclaimed without distortion, it is still the voice of God (Hebrews 4:6, 7).

The capacity for something more is available in the context of our Bible studies and preaching environments. These are sacred places that Jesus would fill with life, instruction, insight, and guidance. But we have treated these places casually and academically and many times, rebelliously. How many preachers have become the Sunday turkey for many Christians following the service as they feast upon the blessing of God? Rather than marching off to church to fulfill our duty, we should assess the spiritual environment we are entering. Jesus is present both by promise and through the praises of his people. His confirmed written Scripture is about to be taught and proclaimed. The preacher has wrestled with and prayed over the text. The people are coming together asking God to bless the preacher and give them encouragement and direction in life. The stage is set for God to speak. "Today, if you hear his voice, do not harden your hearts."

God does a lot of talking in the preaching. As a preacher, it used to trouble me at times—when I listened to people following the morning service—how people seemed to take away from the message of the day something far different than what I thought I preached. I have always had this tendency to correct the record. But I have learned that everyone comes to this sacred environment with different needs, trials, and concerns. Somehow, through whatever the message may be for the day, people hear God speaking to them. But you must be present to hear him talking! He makes the word come alive for every person who is inclined to receive and obey.

The preaching environment is not a classroom setting, but a place that God occupies in order to speak to his people. And yes, he may just have something to say through the preacher! I am confident that when we begin to see our gatherings on Sunday as the active environment that it really is, we will hear a lot more from God. He has designed it that way. It simply requires a prayerful preacher, a prayerful congregation, and hearts inclined to obey. I think that God shows up for that! We may even hear his voice!

## A New Day of Prophesying

We live in a different environment than the saints of the Old Testament. Referring back to the heroes of faith listed in Hebrews 11, the writer states: "These were all commended for their faith, yet none of them received what had been promised. God had planned something better for us so that only together with us would they be made perfect" (Hebrews 11:39, 40). This echoes something similar to what Peter said concerning the Old Testament prophets who "searched intently and with the greatest care, trying to find out the time and circumstances to which the Spirit of Christ in them was pointing when he predicted the sufferings of Christ and the glories that would follow" (1 Peter 1:10, 11). We now live with the things that they longed to see "told to us" (1 Peter 1:12).

We live with a new confidence. Paul tells us that "he made known to us the mystery of his will according to his good pleasure, which he purposed in Christ to be put into effect when the times reach their fulfillment—to bring unity to all things in heaven and on earth under Christ" (Ephesians 1:9, 10). Whereas in the past the prophets held some pieces to the puzzle not knowing how they fit together, now all the pieces have been connected together in Christ. The mystery is solved in Christ and is now being put into effect "with a view to an administration suitable to the fullness of the times" or literally "a stewardship" of the fullness of times (Ephesians 1:10, NASB) Paul understands this stewardship to be the church. He states that a part of his own calling involved making plain to everyone "the administration (stewardship) of this mystery, which for ages past was kept hidden in God, who created all things. His intent was that now, through the church, the manifold wisdom of God should be made known to the rulers and authorities in the heavenly realms, according to his eternal purpose that he accomplished in Christ Jesus our Lord" (Ephesians 3:9–11).

Paul's writing presents us with two interconnected understandings. We don't live with pieces of the puzzle anymore, but with the completed picture of

God's purposes. This is the fullness of times, and we have insight into matters previously locked in mystery. These matters involve things accomplished in Jesus. And not only do we have insight, we are on the move with Jesus in "summing up all things in Christ, (literally "to bring together under one head") things in the heavens and things upon the earth" (NASB). What Paul presents sounds much like the vivid description John presents in Revelation concerning activities both in heaven and on earth. Heaven is buzzing, and the whole universe is caught up in the drama.

Something happened! With the resurrection of Jesus, all of heaven broke loose. Jesus is alive. "See, the Lion of the tribe of Judah, the Root of David, has triumphed!" (Revelation 5:5). And after his ascension to heaven, they are singing a new song to him. "You are worthy to take the scroll and to open its seals, because you were slain, and with your blood you purchased for God members of every tribe and language and people and nation. You have made (made now?) them to be a kingdom and priests to serve our God, and they will reign (or are reigning) on the earth" (Revelation 5:9, 10). There is a drama played out here that involves us presently. We should notice that the twenty-four elders who fell down before the Lamb were holding "golden bowls full of incense, which are the prayers of the saints" (Revelation 5:8). John also sees in this picture all of God's saints and creatures, whether "in heaven and on earth and under the earth and on the sea" (Revelation 5:13) worshipping the Lamb. All of this is brought to focus in Jesus and the events that unfolded in Jerusalem during the final week of his ministry.

None of what is described in Revelation happened by chance. It couldn't be more striking than what we read concerning John's own commission as given to him by Jesus. He was to write what he saw. At the end of this writing, Jesus then says to him: "Do not seal up the words of the prophecy of this scroll, because the time is near" (Revelation 22:10). How dramatically different is this instruction as compared to that given to Daniel at the close of his prophecy. Here is how it is stated: "But you, Daniel, close up and seal the words of the scroll until the time of the end … Go your way, Daniel, because the words are closed up and sealed until the time of the end" (Daniel 12:4, 9). In the Old Testament, the instruction is to seal the words and lay them up for a distant future. But with Revelation, it is not the time to seal, but to open and read and proclaim. The lid has been removed.

We live in an active time involving things in heaven and things on earth. Jesus is alive and active, working out his plan through the church to bring all things, whether in heaven or on earth, under one head. He lives to answer our prayers. He lives to empower his word. It is a word unsealed, living, and active now! It is the making of an environment in which God is still talking. Are we listening?

# Chapter 3

# IT'S GOING TO GET CRAZY

I listened to my parents say it. Now my own children hear me repeating it. They may not want to believe that it is going to happen to them, but it will. They will say something like this to their children: "When I was a child, we would …" We romanticize about those days long ago when we believed that life was better and surer. The problem is that if we were honest, not too many of us want to go back to those times. The memories warm our hearts. But I sort of like my two bathrooms instead of one and my shower on the same floor instead of in the basement and two cars so that I am not stuck when one of them breaks down. And is there anybody who would like to go back to the old clickity typewriter? I love editing this manuscript as a word document as opposed to the prospect of re-typing an actual paper document sent by snail mail!

Christians do this all the time when we study the Bible. We read about the heroes of the faith and reflect on the marvelous miracles that God performed for them. All of that causes us to yearn for the ancient days when God was so active. Who wouldn't want to experience God parting the Red Sea, or who wouldn't want to be one of the disciples who watched Jesus walk on water? We feel like ones who are untimely born.

Where are the miracles? Why doesn't Jesus just appear and make himself plain before the eyes of everyone to see? (Duh, when that happens, it's over!) If only Jesus would part the cars on the Long Island Expressway, how much bolder I would become in my faith! There seems to be a lot of pining for the old days without really knowing what that means.

The signs, miracles, and wonders of God didn't seem to accomplish all that much in the past. The Israelites murmured in the midst of God's wonders and died in the wilderness. Elijah dramatically defeated the prophets of Baal before the eyes of the people, but the nation still followed after the gods of the surrounding peoples. Jesus performed miracle after miracle before the Jewish leaders, but they plotted his death just the same. The rich man, Lazarus, who was in torment in Hades, believed that if someone from the dead would go to his family, they would repent. Abraham responded: "If they do not listen to Moses and the Prophets, they will not be convinced even if someone rises from the dead" (Luke 16:31). No truer word has ever been spoken!

Let's face the truth. Yearning for the days of miracles would not make one ounce of difference in our life. The track record of people in the past provides adequate proof. How is it that we Christians, who live in the new age of promise, get so trapped in dead end, limited thinking? How do we not see the wonder of our own time? (Maybe it takes another book to answer those questions, but I surmise that it would be a lot of complaining.)

We need to adjust to the truth that we are not left out of the adventure. Did not Jesus say to his disciples: "Very truly I tell you, *all who have faith in me* will do the works I have been doing, and they will do even greater things than these, because I am going to the Father" (John 14:12). And we are in the company of those after the resurrection, to whom Jesus pronounced the blessing: "Blessed are those who have not seen and yet have believed" (John 20:29).

It is a funny thing. The Old Testament prophets yearned for the times of the last days. We seem to be lost in some seminar of their days. We are like strangers in the night bypassing one another without a connection.

I don't know about you, but I enjoy thinking about the prophets longing for the last days because they seemed to know that it was going to get a little crazy!

## "Thy Kingdom Come"

It happened on the day of Pentecost, one of the three major festivals of the Jews. The people gathered around the apostles after witnessing a strange phenomenon. They derided the apostles as having too much wine. Peter stood up with the rest of the apostles and announced that they just witnessed what Joel spoke about: "In the last days, God says, I will pour out my Spirit on all people" (Acts 2:17). We encountered this phrase "in the last days" in the opening words of Hebrews. The last days were associated with the Son. Here Peter connects the last days to the effusion of the Spirit on all people. These are two major indicators of the last times and the entrance of the kingdom of God that the prophets heralded.

In Jesus' day, people were looking for this kingdom. Remember Simeon and Anna. Both of these people saw Jesus when he was consecrated in the temple. Luke records that Simeon "was waiting for the consolation of Israel" (Luke 2:25) and that Anna "spoke about the child to all who were looking forward to the redemption of Jerusalem" (Luke 2:38). And remember Joseph of Arimathea who went to Pilate to ask for the body of Jesus. Luke says about him that "he himself was waiting for the kingdom of God" (Luke 23:51). And then there is Jesus' encounter with the two men on their way to Emmaus. Jesus wanted to know what they were discussing. They were surprised that Jesus did not seem to be aware of the things that had happened in Jerusalem concerning Jesus of Nazareth. They explained: "He was a prophet, powerful in word and deed before God and all the people. The chief priests and our rulers handed him over to be sentenced to death, and they crucified him; but we had hoped that he was the one who was going to redeem Israel" (Luke 24:19–21).

We can also place the disciples in the camp of those who were waiting. They were given more by Jesus, but still seemed slow to understand. After Jesus' resurrection, he presented himself to the disciples, appearing to them over a period of forty days. Luke says that he "was speaking about the kingdom of God" (Acts 1:3). He also told them to go into Jerusalem and wait, for in a few days they would be baptized in the

Holy Spirit. They put two and two together—teaching about the kingdom and the baptism of the Holy Spirit, and asked Jesus this question: "Lord, are you at this time going to restore the kingdom to Israel?" (Acts 1:6).

It is an appropriate question. But it also betrayed the limitation of their insight. Like the rest of the people, the disciples had a narrow view of Israel's rule. They were not prepared for how crazy or how big it was going to get! A large dose of the Spirit would be required to remove the cobwebs.

## Bits and Pieces of the Last Days

The last days are an Old Testament concept that evolved in God's dealings with his own people, the nation of Israel. Closely associated with it is another phrase, "the Day of the Lord." From Israel's perspective, it referred to a time of justice and righteousness when God would show himself as victor over the world, vindicating his claims to be the Lord over all the earth. The nation of Israel would rise to prominence over the nations. It would be a day that the Messiah stepped in to set up his kingdom rule over the world through Israel.

The Old Testament prophets present a mixed picture of these days. It befuddled Amos that Israel yearned for the day of the Lord. He writes: "Woe to you who long for the day of the Lord! Why do you long for the day of the Lord? That day will be darkness, not light" (Amos 5:18). In another place, he writes: "In that day, declares the Sovereign Lord,

I will make the sun go down at noon and darken the earth in broad daylight. I will turn your religious festivals into mourning and all your singing into weeping" (Amos 8:9, 10) Yet on the other hand, Amos declares God saying: "In that day I will restore David's fallen shelter—I will repair its broken walls and restore its ruins and will rebuild it as it used to be ... I will plant Israel in their own land, never again to be uprooted from the land I have given them" (Amos 9:11, 15).

Isaiah also addressed God's judgment on Israel, but gave this description for those who "walk in the light of the Lord" (Isaiah 2:5). He writes:

> In the last days the mountain of the Lord's temple will be established as the highest of the mountains; it will be exalted above the hills, and all nations will stream to it. Many peoples will come and say, "Come, let us go up to the mountain of the Lord, to the house of the God of Jacob. He will teach us his ways, so that we may walk in his paths." The law will go out from Zion, the word of the Lord from Jerusalem."
>
> Isaiah 2:2, 3

Micah, a contemporary of Isaiah, says the same thing in nearly the exact same words (Micah 4:1ff).

As the concept and picture continued to get filled out in time, the last days, or the day of the Lord, became associated with a future to be inaugurated with the coming of the Messiah. "For unto us a child is born, to us a son is given, and the government will be on his shoulders. And he will be called Wonderful,

Counselor, Mighty God, Everlasting Father, Prince of Peace. Of the increase of his government and peace there will be no end" (Isaiah 9:6, 7). Isn't this enough to get one's heart racing and yearning for the day of the Lord? Who wouldn't want the Mighty God stepping in and leading triumphantly to better days? Who wants to go back to the good old days?

But as one studies all the Old Testament prophets, a person must admit that it is a pretty wild ride sorting through all of it. I liken it to a ride in Wildwood, New Jersey when I was a kid. It was called the Wild Mouse. It didn't look like much from the ground. It wasn't as high as a roller coaster. It seemed to move slowly through its course. But it was out there on the edge of the pier looking down at the waves. As it moved across the top level, all one could see was the ocean. It would move toward the ocean as if it were not going to stop. At the last moment, just as you believed that you were going to go off the edge, it would jerk to a new direction. That's why they called it the Wild Mouse! I have never ridden a ride like it to this day.

It gets a little crazy putting together the pieces of the last days. It twists and turns us in all directions. But Peter raises the issue and seems to link Joel's prophecy with the events on the day of Pentecost in 33 AD. And there is stuff in that prophecy that bears upon the subject of this book. Does Peter help us put the bits and pieces together? Has it happened? Have the last days begun? Are we living in the times of the end? If so, what does it mean, and is it glorious?

# Bigger and Better Things: Acts 2:1–21

The day of Pentecost caught everyone by surprise. Luke tells us that the disciples were gathered together. If they were following the pattern described just after Jesus ascended, they were likely praying. All of a sudden a loud sound, like a violent wind, came blowing into their house. And it was loud; make no mistake about it. Other people in Jerusalem heard it, and they came together in bewilderment. And not only was there a loud sound, but "tongues of fire" over top each disciple. This is starting to remind me of the Wild Mouse!

It is important to note that people "from every nation under heaven" were in Jerusalem (Isaiah 2:2). The crowd of God-fearing Jews who gathered around the disciples heard them talking in their own language. "We hear them declaring the wonders of God in our own tongues!" (Isaiah 2:3). Luke notes: "Amazed and perplexed, they asked one another, 'What does this mean'?" (Acts 2:12). They were also amazed that all the ones who were speaking were Galileans.

God-fearing Jews would be amazed by such a phenomenon. They are witnessing twelve Galileans speaking the wonders of God. This does not accord with their understanding of prophesying. Prophesying was limited to a select few for brief periods of time.

There is a revealing account found in the book of Numbers that highlights this truth. It happened at a time when the congregation of Israel was complaining to Moses about their hardships in the wilderness.

This led to Moses complaining to God, since Moses carried the burden of the people, being the liaison between them and God. Here is what unfolds:

> So Moses went out and told the people what the Lord had said. He brought together seventy of their elders and had them stand around the tent. Then the Lord came down in the cloud and spoke with him, and he took some of the power of the Spirit that was on him and put it on the seventy elders. When the Spirit rested on them, they prophesied—but did not do so again.
>
> However, two men, whose names were Eldad and Medad, had remained in the camp. They were listed among the elders, but did not go out to the tent. Yet the Spirit also rested on them, and they prophesied in the camp. A young man ran and told Moses, "Eldad and Medad are prophesying in the camp."
>
> Joshua son of Nun, who had been Moses' aide since youth, spoke up and said, "Moses, my lord, stop them!"
>
> But Moses replied, "Are you jealous for my sake? I wish that all the Lord's people were prophets and that the Lord would put his Spirit on them!' Then Moses and the elders of Israel returned to the camp."
>
> *Numbers 11:24–30*

It made Joshua a little uncomfortable that others might be speaking on behalf of God. It was a little disconcerting for the people in Israel to see Galileans filled with the Spirit. Their reaction to the disciples reflects their avoidance of the obvious: "Some made fun of them and said, 'They have had too much wine'" (Acts 2:13). It seems we wrestle with the same discomfort when we examine some of the details of Peter's explanation of this event.

Peter links this phenomenon with the last days and the "pouring out of God's Spirit on all people" (Acts 2:17). What God demonstrated in the disciples wasn't going to stop. "Your sons and daughters will prophesy" (Acts 2:17). And it would not stop with them. It would extend beyond them to everyone: "And everyone who calls on the name of the Lord will be saved" (Acts 2:21). Peter's use of Joel's prophecy served as the introduction to the first gospel message proclaiming Jesus as Lord and Christ. "The law will go out from Zion, the word of the Lord from Jerusalem" (Isaiah 2:3) and "You will be my witnesses in Jerusalem, and in all Judea and Samaria, and to the ends of the earth" (Acts 1:8).

Peter announces the dawning of a glorious new day. All the pieces come together in this Messianic era that stretches between two comings. It involves the generosity of God's gift that would be distributed to all people. There is no limitation in age, sex, or status! The last days have begun. The age of the Spirit is upon us. He has been poured out. God has opened the spigots. The word is out, and God is talking up a storm through an expanded host of his people. The heavens have been shaken, and the end of an era with all its attendant institutions is gone (cp Acts 2:19, 20 with Amos 8:9, 10). It's time to join the adventure!

## Stuck in Neutral

Not everyone sees Joel's prophecy in the same way. Some commentators take the view that Peter did not say that Pentecost was the fulfillment of Joel's prophecy. They believe that the prophecy deals specifically with Israel in the end times. Peter was simply led to see some application to the church. Others comment that Pentecost fulfilled what Joel described but Acts 2:19, 20 was not fulfilled. In this view, there is still some waiting to do with regard to the millennial kingdom of the future.

There is general agreement that prophesying took place in the early church, but that it was limited. It was still a ministry that belonged to a select few despite what Joel said. Moses longed for the day that "all the Lord's people were prophets." Why are we inclined toward the opposite viewpoint when there is this new age when "your sons and daughters will prophesy, your young men will see visions, your old men will dream dreams" (Acts 2:17)? And in regard to the mention of visions and dreams, those belong to the camp of exceptions to the rule—archaic relics of the past that sometimes happened. These are not means of communication that we should expect to happen to us today. Did widespread prophesying, visions, and dreams pass away at the end of the first century, or was Pentecost just the beginning of God opening the spigot?

It is no wonder that a student of this passage becomes immobilized and bored after consulting the commentaries. The results of one's study consist of a whole lot of unconnected pieces scattered all over the counter after the commentators have sliced and diced the passage. It leaves one wondering what is left here for us to chew on and apply to our life now.

It is a strange place to find ourselves as Christians. On the one hand, there are those around us who yearn for the ancient days when God seemed so active and dramatic. On the other hand, there are those who are like the Old Testament prophets, who searched intently the pieces revealed to them, wanting to know the completed picture. We have plenty of Christians whose sights are set on the future day when Jesus comes back. These two opposite poles of thought leave a host of Christians caught in the middle, bored and waiting, stuck in neutral.

Simeon seemed to have sorted it all out and found what he was looking for. Seeing Jesus and taking him into his arms, Simeon praised God saying, "Sovereign Lord, as you have promised, you may now dismiss your servant in peace. For my eyes have seen your salvation, which you have prepared in the sight of all nations: a light for revelation to the Gentiles, and the glory of your people Israel" (Luke 2:29–32).

It's time to live in the now and join God's exciting journey. Too many of us are still waiting for God to do something wonderful. Well he has! He has established an administration for these very times, the church, and poured out His Spirit in us. His Spirit serves to communicate the guidance and purposes of God to us. He is active in us. (Maybe even a little crazy?) So Paul can write this benediction for all of us: "May the grace of the Lord Jesus Christ, and the love of God, and the communion of the Holy Spirit be with you all" (2 Corinthians 13:14). And he is communing with us! How much are we missing?

**Chapter 4**

# INSIDE OUT

Wouldn't you just like to know what she is thinking? That was a common question asked recently by my family when we enjoyed sharing time with Aubree, the newest member of our family (my granddaughter. I'm old). She isn't talking yet. But you know she is thinking. It is that impish look that just melts you.

Aubree saw a speaker wire that I had tucked into the carpet along the wall. It got the best of her curiosity. Before anyone could do anything about it, the wire was all pulled out. It is that turn-around look that makes you wonder what she is thinking, for she turns around to see if anyone noticed and if it has any consequences. You would just enjoy knowing what is occurring in that developing mind. If only she could state her thoughts, it might be even more amusing. But you would have to be inside to know!

In the financial world, they call them insiders. Insiders are the people who are in the company. They buy and sell the stock that affects how others assess the stability of the company. Outsiders depend on secondhand information. The insiders are better positioned, qualified, and informed to make decisions. They have access to information that the rest of us do not possess. They have established communication channels to get that information to the inside people. Thus, they have an advantage in making money or deceiving the general public. It is better to be on the inside!

Moses was an insider. The relationship between God and Moses is really quite incredible to ponder. God told Moses, "I am going to come to you in a dense cloud, so that the people will hear me speaking with you and will always put their trust in you" (Exodus 19:9). In another place, it is recorded: "The Lord would speak to Moses face to face, as one speaks to a friend" (Exodus 33:11). Can you imagine?

Jesus was all about the inside. Christians immediately think about Jesus' teaching about the heart in response to the Pharisees challenge concerning the disciples eating with unwashed hands. Defilement originates from the heart (Matthew 15:1–20). And we recall the contrasts he made in the Sermon on the Mount between what the law said and what the deeper truth involved. But have we given as much thought to the powerfully positive promise he made concerning the Spirit? John records:

> On the last and greatest day of the Festival, Jesus stood and said in a loud voice, "Let *anyone* who is thirsty come to me and drink. *Whoever believes in me,* as Scripture has said, rivers of living water will flow from within them." By this he meant the Spirit, whom those who believed in him were later to receive. Up to that time the Spirit had not been given, since Jesus had not yet been glorified.
>
> John 7:37–39

There is a whole lot more going on inside! Access, information, communication—it's all about getting connected to the innermost chambers of thinking.

## God Is All About the Inside

Remember the famous words of Moses given to his people as a memorial for all their generations? Here is what he wrote:

> Hear, O Israel: The Lord our God, the Lord is one. Love your God with all your heart and with all your soul and with all your strength. These commandments that I give you today are to be on your hearts. Impress them on your children. Talk about them when you sit at home and when you walk along the road, when you lie down and when you get up. Tie them as symbols on your hands and bind them on your foreheads. Write them on the doorframes of your houses and on your gates.
>
> *Deuteronomy 6:4–9*

Moses paints this beautiful portrait of God's people totally immersed in God. He pictures every nook and cranny of one's life breathing God, both inside and out and everywhere a person might look. In this picture, this love relationship to God would be passed from generation to generation, a love relationship that is deep and forever. Except that in time, something went askew.

The reality that persisted for centuries presented a different picture. Jesus quoted Isaiah saying to the Pharisees and teachers of the law in his day: "Isaiah was right when he prophesied about you hypocrites; as it is written, 'These people honor me with their lips, but their hearts are far from me. They worship me in vain; their teachings are merely human rules'" (Mark 7:6, 7). The love and devotion that the people professed did not coincide with their true relationship to God. They were not walking in lockstep with the laws, teaching, precepts, and guidance of God.

In Jesus' day, some sects among the Jews took the words of Moses a little more literally than he intended. Referring to the teachers of the law and the Pharisees, Jesus pointed out to the crowds: "Everything they do is done for people to see: They make their phylacteries wide and the tassels on their garments long" (Matthew 23:5). A phylactery consisted of a case that enclosed four texts of Scripture. This case was fastened by certain straps to the forehead just between the eyes. Another form of the phylactery consisted of two rolls of parchment on which the same texts were written, enclosed in a case of black calfskin. This was worn on the left arm near the elbow. For the ultra pious, enlarging the phylacteries showed their adherence to the teachings of God. Except their "hearts were far from" him.

We have our own ways to display our piety. We enlarge our Bibles, place them on our coffee tables, and dust them off when company comes. We turn our cars into moving billboards for Jesus: "Honk if you love Jesus," "Repent or perish!" "If you see this car unattended …" The fish symbol is a little less offensive.

I suppose there is nothing wrong with any of this until some car cuts us off at an intersection. None of our symbols or bumper stickers can hold back our words or gestures. We wear symbols around our necks and display black ashes on the forehead during the Lenten season. Recently, one lady was seen in a grocery store having ashes on her head while she cursed out the cashier. It can be a little comical at times, except for the reality. The displays of our piety and the true condition of our lives don't agree for a large population of Christians.

It is not the vision God has in mind for his people, whom he desires "for the display of his splendor" (Isaiah 61:3). So he promised a better way, a new relationship to his people. Here is how he describes it through Jeremiah:

> "The days are coming," declares the Lord, "when I will make a new covenant with the house of Israel and with the house of Judah. It will not be like the covenant I made with their ancestors when I took them by the hand to lead them out of Egypt, because they broke my covenant, though I was a husband to them," declares the Lord. "This is the covenant I will make with the house of Israel after that time," declares the Lord. "I will put my law in their minds and write it on their hearts. I will be their God and they will be my people. No longer will they teach their neighbors, or say to one another, "Know the Lord,' because they will all know me, from the least of them to the greatest."

> Jeremiah 31:31–34

Ezekiel also speaks to that time when God promised: "I will give you a new heart and put a new spirit *in you;* I will remove from you your heart of stone and give you a heart of flesh. And I will put my Spirit *in you* and move you to follow my decrees and be careful to keep my laws" (Ezekiel 36:26, 27).

In God's new relationship to his people, it is all about knowing, teaching, and moving from the inside out!

## The New Covenant of the Spirit

What a super picture Paul draws of the Corinthians and all people who turn to the Lord. In his second letter to the Corinthian Christians, Paul states: "You yourselves are our letter, written on our hearts, known and read by everyone. You show that you are a letter from Christ, the result of our ministry, written not with ink but with the Spirit of the living God, not on tablets of stone but on *tablets of human hearts*" (2 Corinthians 3:2, 3). Here is a church that is a direct fulfillment of the promise of God.

Paul said concerning himself and the others who were a part of his ministry that God "made us competent as ministers of a new covenant, not of the letter but of the Spirit" (2 Corinthians 3:6). In 2 Corinthians 3, he compares this new covenant with the old that came through Moses. Here is a listing of words that describe this new covenant: confidence, competence, life, glory, lasts, hope, boldness, freedom, transformation! Now if this description applied to only Paul and his companions, it might not be such a super picture.

They would be the only ones on the inside track with God. But Paul explains that the Corinthians, and even those of us today, are included in this picture.

Moses had a direct connection to God. But when he would come from the presence of God to speak to the people, he would "put a veil over his face to prevent the Israelites from seeing the end of what was passing away" (2 Corinthians 3:13). The problem was not Moses but the Israelites. Paul says their "minds were dull" (2 Corinthians 3:14). The veil over the face of Moses indicated their intimate separation from God. They were more comfortable with Moses as an intermediary. But that simply was a ruse for their rebellious hearts.

What is sadder than their rebellious heart is the glory they missed. God promises a life from the inside with knowledge, instruction, and the residence of his Spirit. He provides a life that is more abundant and free and glorious. God sets that before all of us and provides the means to attain. "But whenever *anyone* turns to the Lord, the veil is taken away" (2 Corinthians 3:16). No longer is any intermediary necessary for any of us. No longer is it just Paul or the apostles or the companions of the apostles that have direct access to God. Everyone is invited to live in the picture of the new covenant, to be transformed, and to contemplate the Lord's glory.

## Living Inside Out

I wonder about us today. Do we get it? Are we living in the full measure of the Spirit available to us? Are we bold, confident, and competent in our ministry? Do we live in hope and freedom? Do we sense the glory that belongs to us? Do we see and possibly hear the Lord? I believe that God would want us to answer all of these questions in the affirmative. His promise and intention in this new covenant relationship to him is that we live in the fullness of the Spirit.

We are insiders now. Jesus entered heaven with his own blood. On the basis of that truth and reality, the Hebrew writer states:

> Therefore, brothers and sisters, since we have confidence to enter the Most holy Place by the blood of Jesus, by a new and living way opened for us through the curtain, that is, his body, and since we have a great priest over the house of God, let us draw near to God with a sincere heart in full assurance of faith, having our hearts sprinkled to cleanse us from a guilty conscience and having our bodies washed with pure water.
>
> Hebrews 10:19–22

We have uninhibited access to God, to the throne room of heaven. There is an open invitation to enter at any time. God desires that we consult with him. But it is even closer than that!

Paul says about all of us: "When you believed, you were marked in him with a seal, the promised Holy Spirit, who is a deposit guaranteeing our inheritance until the redemption of those who are God's possession—to the praise of his glory" (Ephesians 1:13, 14). These Scriptures give us confidence about our eternal life. But it goes beyond that. This is the promise of the new covenant that God would come to take residence in our hearts. Paul said specifically: "I have been crucified with Christ and I no longer live, but *Christ lives in me*" (Galatians 2:20). How much closer can God get?

According to God's promise, he would move within us to keep his ways; he would write his laws on our hearts, and he would teach us to know him. "As for you, the anointing you received from him remains in you, and you do not need anyone to teach you. But as his anointing teaches you about all things and as that anointing is real, not counterfeit—just as it has taught you, remain in him" (1 John 2:27). That's learning and growing and hearing from the inside out. It is the place that God chooses to speak to us intimately. Have we trained our ears to be sensitive to his speaking?

# Chapter 5

# DO WE HAVE THE MIND OF CHRIST?

It occurred in a seminary-level class. I don't recall the course that led us to this Scripture in 1 Corinthians 2. But I remember that it stirred up some great discussion and even some passion. I wish I could recall the culprit who disrupted a rather calm class.

The professor flatly and dogmatically stated his position on the Scripture. He really left no room for any other conclusion. Paul concluded a line of reasoning with the words: "But we have the mind of Christ" (1 Corinthians 2:16). This is a rather startling statement if one ponders it. Is Paul saying that there are people who have the mind of Christ? What a bold claim! This is not something for the timid.

The issue immediately centers on the word "we." What is the antecedent of the word "we?" To whom is Paul referring when he claims that some have the mind of Christ? The professor made it plain, without discussion (well, some discussion followed) that the word referred to none other than the apostles. They are the only ones who possess the mind of Christ.

This conclusion naturally leads to the question, "Where do the rest of us fit?" When we, in all our ways, acknowledge God and seek him in prayer for guidance, how does he give that direction? How does he answer that prayer? Where do we go to determine the mind of Jesus in matters not specifically addressed in the written record of the apostles? How does God talk to us?

What one determines about the word "we" carries great impact for a person's relationship to God and for this book. If the apostles are the sole possessors of the mind of Christ, they must then become the mediators through whom all the rest of us receive direction. But if "we" refers to a broader group of individuals, then a different dynamic comes into play. Is it possible that any of us living in the twenty-first century could be included in "we?" Is there any possibility that Christians today—in seats of our churches—could have "the mind of Christ" apart from the words of Scripture? Determining the answer to that question requires tracing the inclusive pronouns in 1 Corinthians chapters 1 and 2. This chapter requires that you open your Bibles and follow the references.

## Who Is "We?"

Paul wrote, "We have the mind of Christ" (1 Corinthians 2:16). This verse concludes a section of this letter that goes back to chapter one beginning at verse 10. Paul appeals to the Corinthians to agree with one another—to be "perfectly united in mind and thought" (1 Corinthians 1:10). He makes this appeal because he received information from Chloe's household that quarrels existed among the Corinthians. He explains what these quarrels involved. People in the church began to cluster around certain leaders who were preachers or teachers of the gospel. Paul names these leaders: Paul, Apollos, Cephas, Christ. Are these the ones to whom the word "we" refer? It could be, and if it does, there are leaders on this list who are not apostles. (Remember, I was taught in class that "we have the mind of Christ" refers to the apostles.) Apollos was not an apostle. And the reference to Christ most likely refers to a leader who possibly claimed to teach more purely the teachings of Christ. And there is no indication that Cephas (Peter) had anything to do with the church in Corinth unless it refers to some leader who claimed to be schooled under Peter.

"We" must have an antecedent. To whom does it make reference? Navigating the "we" and "us" trail to the end of 1 Corinthians 2 is not easy. But it is important that we make some attempt toward a reasonable opinion.

In 1 Corinthians 1:18, Paul begins his reasoning about the central and primary significance of the cross, writing "For the message of the cross is foolishness to those who are perishing, but to *us* who are being saved it is the power of God." As opposed to the importance of the teachers of the church, Paul states squarely that it is the message of the cross that possesses power. The word "us" would be inclusive of both the hearers and the preachers since it embodies people who are contrasted with another group "who are perishing" and who are labeled as foolish.

Continuing on to verses 22 and 23, Paul states, "Jews demand signs and Greeks look for wisdom, but *we* preach Christ crucified." To whom does the "we" refer here? Is it just the apostles? Is it a reference to the named leaders of the Corinthian church? Is it applicable to anyone in the church who has the role of preaching the gospel? There is no direct antecedent to this pronoun except those mentioned in verse 12. That group includes the names of people who were not apostles. We assume that all of them taught the same central message of Christ crucified.

Moving to chapter 2, Paul makes some direct application to himself: "And so it was with me, brothers and sisters. When I came to you, I did not come with eloquence or human wisdom as I proclaimed to you the testimony about God" (1 Corinthians 2:1). Paul makes reference to his own approach to preaching that involved simply presenting "Jesus Christ and him crucified" (1 Corinthians 2:2). It is important to note that the preachers and teachers in Corinth were not the problem. All presented the same message. The division in the church arose from the people who elevated the leaders to positions of superior knowledge and eloquence. The Corinthian Christians were stumbling back to a wisdom of words that involved a worldly standard. Paul lumps all of that together as "foolishness."

Then verse 6 begins two long sections involving "we" and "us" and "our." This requires that we look at each section in its entirety. Navigating this as correctly as possible brings us nearer to the answer of who is meant when Paul writes that "We have the mind of Christ."

So let's look at section one.

*We* do, however, speak a message of wisdom among the mature, but not the wisdom of this age or of the rulers of this age, who are coming to nothing. No, *we* declare God's wisdom, a mystery that has been hidden and that God destined for *our* glory before time began. None of the rulers of this age understood it, for if they had, they would not have crucified the Lord of glory. However, as it is written: "What no eye has seen, what no ear has heard, and what no human mind has conceived—these things God has prepared for those who love him"—for God has revealed them to *us* by his Spirit.

2 Corinthians 2:6–10

This section confronts us with a series of inclusive pronouns: we, our, and us. And there are two other significant phrases that awaken our attention: "among the mature" and "those who love him." Who are these people, and how do they figure into the inclusive pronouns?

Paul says, "*We* speak." Tracing his line of reasoning, I believe we must conclude that the "we" refers to the same people to whom he refers in chapter one verses 22 and 23. These would be the people who are teaching and announcing the gospel. This message is presented to the "mature." In this context, the mature are those who are unlike the rulers of the age who "crucified the Lord of glory." The mature heard the message, received it, and understood it. These people would include the Corinthians and anyone else who responded to the message in the same manner even down to our present time.

This message was destined for "*our* glory." "Our" must refer to both the presenters and the receivers of the message. It is the message that has the power "for *us* who are being saved" (1 Corinthians 1:18). Then Paul quotes Scripture to draw a line of demarcation between the foolish rulers and the mature, adding another characteristic of the mature. The mature are "those who love him (God)." Wonderful things that "no eye has seen and no ear has heard" (1 Corinthians 2:9) are revealed to people who love him. Which brings us to the question, to whom does "*us*" refer at the conclusion of this section when Paul states "for God has revealed them to *us*" (1 Corinthians 2:10)? Are the wonderful things which are revealed given only to the apostles, or does it include the other "preachers" of the message or can it include all of them plus "the mature"—everyone who received the message because they loved the Lord?

This leads us to the final section of this series of inclusive pronouns. The link to this final section is the introduction of the Spirit. God revealed these wonderful things to *us* "by his Spirit." Paul discusses how the Spirit operates in this manner and then writes:

> *We* have not received the spirit of the world, but the Spirit who is from God, that *we* may understand what God has freely given *us*. This is what *we* speak, not in words taught *us* by human wisdom but in words taught by the Spirit, explaining spiritual realities with Spirit-taught words. The person

without the Spirit does not accept the things that come from the Spirit of God but considers them foolishness, and cannot understand them because they are discerned only through the Spirit. The person with the Spirit makes judgments about all things, but such a person is not subject to merely human judgments, for "Who has known the mind of the Lord so as to instruct him?" But *we* have the mind of Christ.

1 Corinthians 2:12–16

So again, we have a series of inclusive pronouns. To whom do these pronouns refer?

Everyone agrees that the phrase "we speak" refers once again to those who taught or preached the message. But what about all the other "we's"? It all depends on who is included in the "us" of verse 10. It is the closest antecedent of the "we" in verse 12. Answering that question requires discussing the function of the Spirit as stated in these verses.

Paul teaches that God revealed his wisdom and the mystery by his Spirit. The Spirit knows the thoughts of God, searching all the deep things of God. The Spirit serves as the means leading to understanding. He provides the words that explain spiritual realities. Those who do not have the spirit regard the teachings as foolishness. They are attempting to understand spiritual realities without the aid of the Spirit. But people who do have the Spirit make judgments about these matters and discern these things. The Spirit gives discernment and judgment. And they live apart from the judgments of others because they have minds that are instructed by the Lord. People who do not know the instruction of Jesus have no standard for judgment. How can others judge the mind of the Lord if they do not have the mind of the Lord? "But *we* have the mind of Christ."

The Spirit of God is the common denominator for both the teachers of the word and the receivers of the word. He knows the deep things of God and reveals those things. The revelation happens through the preaching of the cross by people appointed for that task. People who hear and believe become included in the ongoing revelation of God through his Spirit. People who have his Spirit understand, discern, and make judgments about matters that people without the Spirit cannot in kind do.

In my judgment, the "we" of Paul's concluding statement, "we have the mind of Christ," must be inclusive of not just the apostles, not just the presenters of the message, but also of those who are mature—who understand, who love him, who discern, who judge, who are being saved, who have the Spirit of God.

## The Necessity of the Spirit for Understanding

All three persons of the Godhead converge in this Scripture. It is the Spirit of God who knows the thoughts of God. And the thoughts of God are nothing less than the mind of the Lord, who is Jesus. Paul refers to him as the "Lord of glory" in verse 8 whom the rulers of this world crucified.

God is in the business of making himself and his

truth known. This is the truth that sets the God of the Bible apart from any other gods. He reveals, explains, and teaches spiritual realities. These involve matters that no human mind can conceive.

The difference between those who see, hear, understand, and judge is that the mature—those who love him—have received the "Spirit who is from God." Paul expected the Corinthians to understand and judge correctly his teachings and the teachings of others because they too had the mind of Christ. The Spirit of God is the common, active factor for all Christians.

We have the mind of Christ if we have received his Spirit. This truth gives us confidence in living. There is an active, daily relationship to God that can lead to exploring things no mind has conceived. Now, whether or not we live in that dimension is another matter. Paul was disappointed that the Corinthian Christians were living below that expectation. He wrote: "I could not address you as spiritual but as worldly" (1 Corinthians 3:1).

God is still talking! But are we listening? Are we living in the adventure of a dynamic relationship to God? For Christians, it is not so much a question of the truth that we have the Spirit of God. The problem centers around the question of how we are led by the Spirit of God.

## Chapter 6

# GETTING TO WHERE YOU ARE GOING

In matters not addressed directly and expressly by the Scriptures, all of us want God's direction for what to do or what to decide. How do we know the mind of Christ with regard to matters not addressed in the Scriptures? Does the Scripture give direction for every particular in one's life? And how personal is that? And is it a reasonable expectation? Do the Scriptures give us any reason to believe that we can have some personal guidance from God in our life? We just want to know.

## The Invitation of God

There is a Scripture from Proverbs that Christians know very well. Most Christians have it memorized and can repeat it fluently without difficulty. We print the words across beautiful pictures and tack it to the walls in our homes and churches. We apply it to crisis situations indiscriminately. If we were truthful, it is the crisis situation that usually brings out this Scripture for application. Here it is:

> Trust in the Lord with all your heart and lean not on your own understanding; In all your ways sub-

mit to (acknowledge) Him and He will make your paths straight.

Proverbs 3:5, 6

But God didn't intend for it to be a slogan that has an appealing ring without real substance. It is really an invitation to join him in a daily adventure.

This Scripture breaks down into four natural parts that are to be engaged in the successive order that is stated. And it starts with trust. Now for Christians who have made the decision that Jesus is Lord and Christ, this naturally should be the starting point for our day as we awaken in the morning. We began a new life by placing our faith in him. The constant challenge is to live in that determination throughout the course of our lives. When we were introduced to Jesus, God invited us to put our trust in him. Each day God invites us to stay focused in this decision. "Let us run with perseverance the race marked out for us, fixing our eyes on Jesus, the pioneer (author) and perfecter of our faith" (Hebrews 12:1, 2).

Second, God clearly tells us to lay aside our own understanding when we are living in a relationship with him. Most of us have the problem of wanting or needing to be in control of everything. We tend to trust our own knowledge. It is hard for us to swallow the thought that we don't understand or can't understand everything. Usually, we decide on some course of action without floating it by God and then we want him to cover our tracks. The fact is that God doesn't work the way we work. His thoughts and his ways are higher than ours. We must approach God with the humility of heart to adjust our thoughts and ways if he leads in another direction. Any other approach could cause us to miss the clear direction from God that we are seeking.

Third, there is no holding back with God. Everything that is on our mind can be placed before God. Our hopes, our desires, our plans, our dreams, our present activities—all of that and more can be discussed with him. After all, we are addressing here a personal relationship to God. It is a conversation. He made us in his image for this very reason. We can certainly plan. And he might like what we have planned. It simply involves the discretion to yield to his judgment in the end. If our plans get scuttled, his way is better. We can always be sure of that!

And four, he makes this promise: "I will make your paths straight." I don't know what that means completely. What I do know is that he is in charge of the outcome. It is an adventure. God doesn't always share with us where the path is leading. If we awaken every morning engaging the first three parts of this verse, the rest of the day becomes a surprise. We live with our senses perked up a little higher to see what he has in mind. You just don't know how the day is going to unfold. It sure keeps life from becoming boring.

One of the more remarkable passages of Scripture for me is Mark's accounting of the call of Jesus to Peter, Andrew, James, and John to follow him (Mark 1:16–20). It is an invitation to become involved with Jesus. And we see a real transformation that begins to take shape in the life of these fishermen. They drop everything and follow him. Now, it is important to remind ourselves that this was not their first encounter with Jesus. If we just had Mark's account, we might think that all responses should imitate the response of these disciples. But still, it does not lessen the dramatic action that they took.

Looking at the account as a whole, it unfolds in the following manner. The disciples are faced with the challenge of making some decision about Jesus. Who knows how many times they have heard him or have seen him engage some ministry serving people? But it always starts here—with some decision to place one's faith and trust in him. We can only explain the decision of these disciples on the basis that they found Jesus too compelling to refuse.

And then they must abandon everything on which they had built their life up to that point. They built a business in the fishing industry. But here we see that they leave their nets. It is the challenge to let go, to set aside one's own understanding and to yield in dependence on him. Did they discuss their hopes, dreams, finances, family situation, and a whole lot of other matters with Jesus? I assume they did. We must use our own imagination to construct what Peter must have shared with his wife!

Jesus gives them the promise that they would become fishers of men. Did they know what this would involve? In my opinion, I don't think they had a clue. Jesus invited them to accompany him, to follow him. In the process, they would become something else. There was going to be a change. It would involve a process of becoming. Did they or could they see the final picture of what that would be in its entirety? I believe not. It is simply an invitation to follow, to trust, to leave the results up to him. I will make your paths straight. You might not be able to see where that path is completely going. The only critical component centers on whether or not he is on the path.

God is moving and there is an invitation to join him. It is an invitation extended throughout Scripture.

> Come, all you who are thirsty, come to the water; and you who have no money, come, buy and eat! Come, buy wine and milk without money and without cost. Why spend money on what is not bread, and your labor on what does not satisfy? Listen, listen to me, and eat what is good, and your soul will delight in the richest of fare. Give ear and come to me; hear me, that your soul may live.
>
> Isaiah 55:1–3

> Come to me, all you who are weary and burdened, and I will give your rest. Take my yoke upon you and learn from me, for I am gentle and humble in heart, and you will find rest for your souls. For my yoke is easy and my burden is light.
>
> Matthew 11:28

> Follow me and I will make you become fishers of men.
>
> Mark 1:17

The Spirit and the bride say, "Come!" And let those who hear say, "Come!" Let those who are thirsty come; and let all who wish take the free gift of the water of life.

Revelation 22:17

Call to me and I will answer you and tell you great and unsearchable things you do not know.

Jeremiah 33:3

Would God offer this invitation and not respond? Will he really show us unsearchable things? Is he truly serious about giving personal direction to our lives or are all of these Scriptures just nice-sounding words? And if the invitation is extended to people generally, how much greater is the advantage we possess as Christians?

God gives Christians an edge in living. For Christians to live less than exciting, adventurous, or blessed lives is a real tragedy in light of the fact that we have the all powerful, all-knowing, ever-present God with infinite resources as our Father. There is a new dimension to our life. We have been born again. He has placed his Spirit in us. How much closer can we get to hearing God? He has given the Holy Spirit to us as a gift for the very purpose that we might receive the direction in life that we desire!

# Don't Leave Home Without Him

Where can I go from your Spirit? Where can I flee
from your presence? If I go up to the heavens, you
are there; if I make my bed in the depths, you are
there. If I rise on the wings of the dawn, if I settle
on the far side of the sea, even there your hand will
guide me, your right hand will hold me fast.

Psalm 139:7–10

Guidance is one facet of the ministry of the Holy Spirit.
It is true, in the above Scripture, as a truth sung by the
Hebrew masses. It is true with regard to the promise of Jesus to his disciples when he told them that
the Spirit "will guide you into all truth" (John 16:13).
And it is true with regard to all of us, whether Jew or
Greek, who have been reconciled to God through the
cross. Jesus has become our peace and "through him
we both (Jew and Greek) have access to the Father by
one Spirit" (Ephesians 2:18).

The Holy Spirit is a major player in the book of
Acts, leading and guiding the church in its ministry
to the world. Many commentators believe that Acts
should be titled as the Acts of the Holy Spirit. Jesus
clearly intended that the church would be born and
guided by the Holy Spirit. Be reminded once again
of Jesus' instructions to his disciples just prior to his
ascension:

On one occasion, while he was eating with them,
he gave them this command: "Do not leave Jeru-

salem, but wait for the gift my Father promised, which you have heard me speak about. For John Baptized with water, but in a few days you will be baptized with the Holy Spirit."

Acts 1:4, 5

This is similar to the statement Luke recorded in his gospel: "I am going to send you what my Father has promised; but stay in the city until you have been clothed with power from on high" (Luke 24:49). There was to be no movement until the promise of the Holy Spirit occurred. To think that something as revolutionary as the church could be ignited by twelve ordinary people apart from power from God would be unimaginable.

This is an obvious lesson for the church today. The work of God and the work of his church are not designed to be accomplished by human ingenuity and strength. The Baptist preacher Vance Havner, noted for his pointed and sometimes amusing thoughts, wrote years ago:

> We spend much of our time in church these days trying to work up what is not there. Song leaders try to create a joy the singers do not really feel. Church workers try to create an enthusiasm, a spirit of giving, a love for souls, a zeal for God's house that does not exist. In our desperation we arouse a simulated interest and we become play-actors, pretending what only the Holy Spirit can produce and maintain.[2]

In a more amusing manner, he once said, "Too many church services start at eleven o'clock sharp and end at eleven o'clock dull. The clock struck twelve at Sunday noon and the church gave up her dead."[3]

Jim Cymbala, in his book *Fresh Power* writes:

> The church cannot be the church without the Holy Spirit abiding and empowering it. The degree to which we understand and experience the Spirit of God will be the exact degree to which God's plan for our churches will be accomplished. If we downgrade the Holy Spirit—worse yet, if we ignore him—even worse than that, if we grieve or quench him—we end up with a modern church that is totally foreign to the New Testament.[4]

In his book, he quotes devotional writer William Law from the 1700s on this same subject, who wrote:

> Where the Holy Spirit is not honored as the one through whom the whole life and power of gospel salvation is to be effected, it is no wonder that Christians have no more of the reality of the gospel than the Jews had of the purity of the Law… For the New Testament without the coming of the Holy Spirit in power over self, sin, and the devil is no better a help to heaven than the Old Testament without the coming the Messiah.[5]

The Scripture supports these observations. Paul asks the Corinthians the rhetorical question: "Don't you know that you (plural) yourselves are God's temple and that God's Spirit lives in you?" (1 Corinthians 3:16). Paul expected that they were completely aware of this truth. As applied to our present subject, the Holy Spirit continues to dwell in his church. This is not something solely for the church in the first century. Always and forever, we are a temple, the residence for God's Spirit. He is still directing, guiding, and leading his church.

## Led By the Spirit

Paul teaches rather plainly that "those who are led by the Spirit of God are the children of God" (Romans 8:14). In his letter to the Galatians, he discusses that Christians who walk by the Spirit will not gratify the desires of the sinful nature. He then presents this in a conditional manner stating, "But if you are led by the Spirit, you are not under law" (Galatians 5:18). The phrase that attracts our attention in both Scriptures is "led by the Spirit." The manner in which he puts this forward suggests that this is something Christians would just naturally understand. He offers no explanation of how we are led by the Spirit—a question that constantly gets raised in many Christian circles when this Scripture is discussed. Maybe the question points to the difference between the worldview of Christians living in the first century and their approach to life in contrast to the systematized Christianity we have established and the practical consequence to which it has led.

But let's address the question of "how" we are led by the Spirit for a moment. My own search of a good number of commentaries on this verse probably betrays how I have handled this Scripture in the past.

I went to the commentaries looking for an answer to the how. I want an answer to the question: "How does the Spirit lead us?" Paul teaches in Romans 8 that those who belong to Christ are "in the Spirit" (Romans 8:9) and "are led by the Spirit" (Romans 8:14). Well, what are the specific ways that we are led? Give me a list, or better yet, give me a step-by-step formula that all of us can follow in order to practice being led by the Spirit. Isn't this exactly the driving objective of our question?

Here is the result of this searching. First, there was scant comment on the verse itself. Nearly all the commentators were anxious to expand on the idea of adoption as presented in the verses following verse 14. Second, only one commentator offered any suggestion as to how we are guided or led by the Spirit. His position reflects some of what I have thought, and I am sure that I have presented to people in discussion circles. It basically consists in the view that God guides us by his word day by day. We are led and taught by his word. That almost borders on the written word becoming the replacement for the Spirit in giving us daily guidance. This position makes our life in Christ and in the Spirit more a relationship to the Bible than a relationship to the living God. This is the practical consequence of our scholarship and the science that rules the worldview of our own time. We are more a product on the enlightenment period of history than we are of first century Christianity.

So how do we understand Paul's reference to being led by the Spirit? Commentators agree that it refers to Christians living under the influence of the

Spirit. The core idea in the word "led" is the notion of being guided or taken someplace by another authority, person, or agency. It is to go somewhere under the influence or authority of someone or something else. For example, Luke says concerning Jesus' testing in the wilderness, "Jesus, full of the Holy Spirit, left the Jordan and was led by the Spirit into the wilderness" (Luke 4:1). Later in that chapter, Luke states that "the devil led him to Jerusalem and had him stand on the highest point of the temple" (Luke 4:9). And with regard to Jesus' trial in Jerusalem, John records: "Then the Jewish leaders took (led) Jesus from Caiaphas to the palace of the Roman governor" (John 18:28). In all of these instances, the idea conveyed in the word "led" indicates that Jesus was under the control or influence of another.

So it is the same here in Romans 8. Paul says that "those who live in accordance with the Spirit have their minds set on what the Spirit desires" and that this is equal to a "mind controlled by the Spirit." And a few verses later he writes: "You, however, are not controlled by the sinful nature but are in the Spirit" (Romans 8:5, 6, 9). This whole chapter in Romans is about living under the influence and control of the Spirit. It is the new order of existence into which all who have identified with Jesus in his death and resurrection through baptism have come. It is the realm in which "the law of the Spirit who gives life" (Romans 8:2) is in charge.

So then, how is one led? It is not a question that was asked, let alone answered. The closest answer, if there is one, goes back to Romans chapter 6. Paul commands: "Do not offer any part of yourself to sin as an instrument of wickedness, but rather offer yourself to God as those who have been brought from death to life; and offer every part of yourself to him as an instrument of righteousness" (Romans 6:13). Having come under the control of a new order of life in the Spirit, our active response is to offer or present ourselves to the disposal of God. The King James Version of this uses the word "yield." The idea is to actively, continually, daily, moment by moment place ourselves under the governance and influence of God. It is taking the time every day to check in with God, to recognize his presence, to talk to him, and to align ourselves with his will for that day. Romans 6:13 expresses the whole response to the new order of life to which we have come in Christ.

If we are looking for formulas or lists or a seven-step plan for living under the leadership of the Spirit, we will be greatly disappointed. It just doesn't exist. I believe that it was a foreign concept to these early Christians. They lived in a far more dynamic world of the Spirit. The invisible realities were to be explored and experienced, not analyzed. It was a world of communication, mostly one-dimensional. People had many gods and various avenues of religious activity to inquire of those gods. What changed in Jesus is a God who was really there, who heard, and who answered. Now some real interactive communication could take place.

While there are so many paths that we could take

in this discussion, we must come back to the main point of our thesis. And that is this: God is still talking. It is even more widespread and active, since he now has children who are born again of his Spirit and in whom he has placed his Spirit. And thus we have this beautiful benediction of Paul to the Corinthians at the close of his second letter: "May the grace of the Lord Jesus Christ, and the love of God, and the fellowship of the Holy Spirit be with you all" (2 Corinthians 13:14). The word fellowship is the Greek word "*koinonia*." We translate that word with various English words. In this verse, the King James Version translates it with the word "communion." Using the *Random House Dictionary of the English Language,* we learn that communion is the act of sharing or holding something in common, an interchange or sharing of thoughts or emotions and intimate conversation. Isn't that the kind of relationship we want with God? That when we end the conversation, we depart with confidence in his guidance and direction for our lives!

In closing this chapter, I like the paraphrase of Romans 8:14 as given in *The Message:* "The Spirit beckons. There are things to do and places to go!" Living in a dynamic relationship to God under the influence of his Spirit may just take us places and tell us things to do that the Scripture alone as our guide do not specifically state for each of us personally. Living in the communion of the Holy Spirit requires that we listen and recognize all the ways God may be talking to us. That is the hope in the rest of this book—that we might become aware of the various ways God is talking.

# Chapter 7

# FROM A DISTANCE

We hear the challenge proclaimed. It reverberates in our ears. It is stirring, exciting, and daring. "Follow me!" It is Jesus calling us to ministry, to go where few people go, to rise up and become something that we cannot envision or understand. But it is Jesus issuing the call through Scripture or through some pulpit exposition. If only it were Jesus standing before us, personal, face to face. How differently we would respond! We would rise to the challenge. Or so we think. There were people who heard him and saw him but turned away. "From this time many of his disciples turned back and no longer followed him" (John 6:66). It is not his physical presence that makes the difference.

## A Father-Daughter Dialogue

I was attempting to write this chapter while visiting my daughter Jennifer in Lancaster, Pennsylvania. This chapter was giving me trouble for some reason. I just couldn't get a feel for how to write the thoughts swirling through my mind. I invited her to read my opening paragraphs. After reading them, it was apparent that something wasn't clear. Maybe after you, the readers, get done, it won't be any clearer.

This led to a conversation about having a personal relationship to Christ. What do we mean when we ask someone "Are you having a personal relationship to Christ?" or "Have you accepted Jesus personally?" These are questions that are commonly asked in evangelical circles. Evangelistic outreach seeks to determine whether or not a person has accepted Jesus personally. I have noticed the puzzled look on many people who are confronted with the question. I figured that it was time that we address the question to ourselves.

Jennifer answered the question with some common responses that we give. She talked about reading the Scripture and praying, which are important in our spiritual growth. But how is that personal? Are there not a great number of people who read the Bible and who pray who have not accepted Jesus personally? The fact that we use the question as an evangelistic tool indicates our belief that a person can read and pray but still be separated from Jesus. We believe they need a personal relationship to Christ. What is involved in having a personal relationship?

Jennifer and I attempted to put the question in the context of our relationship. There are different means to having a personal relationship. We see each other occasionally since we no longer live in the same state. So our personal relationship consists of a note or a phone call most of the time. Is that personal? Yes, but just on a different level. No one can argue that seeing each other face to face in the same room, holding a conversation with eye contact and gestures is the ultimate. But the notes and phone calls work from a distance when necessary. It is no less personal. However, it is important to learn that the notes and phone calls are established on a foundation of years of her being my daughter, living in the context of a shared home. She was born into my home, and we got to know one another!

That leaves us with the question of how in our relationship to Christ. How does a person have a personal relationship to someone who is invisible? Is it even possible? Some may even ask, is it necessary? These questions help us probe the thesis of whether or not God is still talking. Maybe the thesis is not disputed. Maybe the real issue involves the personal aspect of that communication. Is there direct, close contact, or is it limited to our study and understanding of Scripture alone?

## Enter, the Bible School Class

"What does it mean to have a personal relationship to Christ?" That was the question presented to my Bible school class one Sunday morning as I was thinking through this chapter. I hadn't planned to ask the question, but something kept prompting me to seek their input. Even with all that prompting, I almost forgot to present the class with the opportunity to respond to the question.

I was surprised by the conversation generated by this question. I expected a few people to share some brief thoughts. I simply wanted to test my suspicions that many Christians are vague about what is meant by this question. Instead of just a few brief responses, the whole class time was consumed by the conversation over this subject. Every person entered the discussion. Contrary to my suspicions, this class seemed to understand clearly the subject matter.

Here are some random thoughts and phrases set forth to define the elements of the question:

Talk to God as I am talking to you

Real time relationship

God and Christ are real

Share celebrations and failures as if talking to my dad

Open and free

Closeness

He's holding on to me

He knows me, as stated in Psalm 139

A relationship that you go through—a process—with trials and hardships at times

One person described a time that he or she was running on empty and was refreshed through prayer. There was no one to lean on at that time but God. It was a deep breath of leaning on God that provided the refreshment. That kind of experience builds a relationship.

Another person spoke about putting God in the middle of all decisions and becoming adapted to his sovereignty. After some time, one is able to look back and see his leading.

Daniella contrasted her relationship to God prior

to being born again. She described her previous relationship to duty, illustrating her point with the task of brushing one's teeth. It is something that you do every night because it is supposed to be done. In her previous religious life, she would pray before she went to bed every night, using the instruments that she was taught to use. She referred to these prayers as empty words. Being born again changed all of this. It was no longer a duty to pray but a refreshing time of knowing that God was there and that he is listening.

How does one define having a personal relationship to Jesus? Someone in the class made the point that the Bible does not specifically talk about this concept. In all the conversation, no one attempted to define an answer to the question. Everyone seemed to understand what was involved. If there is one defining statement that covers all the discussion, it would be this: "Knowing he is there!"

## What Does Jesus Say?

The words of Jesus challenge our concept of having a relationship to him. We spend endless hours, it seems, explaining away some very direct thoughts of Jesus. The following Scriptures record the encouraging words of Jesus given to his disciples in the upper room. Were they just for the disciples, or are we included?

> I will not leave you as orphans; I will come to you. Before long, the world will not see me anymore, but you will see me. Because I live, you also will

live. On that day you will realize that I am in my Father, and you are in me, and I am in you. *Whoever* has my commands and keeps them is the one who loves me. *Anyone* who loves me will be loved by my Father, and I too will love them and show myself to them.

John 14:18–21

*Anyone* who loves me will obey my teaching. My Father will love them, and we will come to them and make our home with them.

John 14:23

My prayer is not for them alone. I pray also for *those who will believe in me* through their message, that *all of them* may be one, Father, just as you are in me and I am in you. *May they also be in us* so that the world may believe that you have sent me.

John 17:20, 21

John understands clearly the teaching contained in Jesus' words and prayer. In his first letter, John writes: "This is how we know that we *live in him and he in us:* He has given us of his Spirit… If *anyone* acknowledges that Jesus is the Son of God, God *lives in them* and they in God" (1 John 4:13, 15).

Paul seems to have gotten it also. We must ponder those familiar words of Paul to the Galatians: "I have been crucified with Christ and I no longer live, but *Christ lives in me.* The life I now live in the body,

I live by faith in the Son of god, who loved me and gave himself for me" (Galatians 2:20). Paul's letters address that same relationship that all of us who have the deposit of the Spirit can experience in our own lives.

We should take at face value the promise: "Come near to God, *and he will come near to you*" (James 4:8). Is it real, or should we fake it and imagine it? It makes a difference in how personal our relationship truly is.

## Closing Thoughts

If we are going to use the terminology of having a personal relationship to Christ, it must be real. If it is a true concept that aligns with the teaching of Scripture, then it presents the possibility that God is still talking and that he is truly listening.

While we might not be able to present a definition that satisfies the concept, Christians who are having a dynamic encounter with God know at least what it is not. It is not something mechanical, performed out of duty or mindless routine. It is not rituals and ceremony or jumping through endless hoops to get to God. "The word is near you; it is in your mouth and in your heart" (Romans 10:8).

How can a person have a personal relationship to someone who is invisible? The answer is "knowing that he is there." Our relationship to people that we love on this earth, but from whom we are separated from a distance, is a limited relationship—a phone call or a letter or a memory. God is bigger than the limitations of this life. He is alive and omnipresent. "Where can

I go from your Spirit? Where can I flee from Your presence? If I go up to the heavens, you are there; if I make my bed in the depths, you are there. If I rise on the wings of the dawn, if I settle on the far side of the sea, even there your hand will guide me, your right hand will hold me fast" (Psalm 139:7–9). Does anyone doubt that God can find a multitude of ways to speak to us, regardless of where we might be?

All of us long for the wonder of that time when we see Jesus face to face. God longs for it also.

> Then I saw a new heaven and a new earth, for the first heaven and the first earth had passed away, and there was no longer any sea. I saw the Holy City, the new Jerusalem, coming down out of heaven from God, prepared as a bride beautifully dressed for her husband. And I heard a loud voice from the throne saying, "Look! God's dwelling place is now among the people, and he will dwell with them. They will be his people, and God himself will be with them and be their God."
>
> Revelation 21:1–3

God desires a relationship with us. It begins now until the day he appears. Let's tune in to hear what he is still speaking.

**Part Two**

# INTRODUCTION

I received an e-mail just this past Tuesday as I was writing another chapter of this book. It came from a wonderful Christian lady who is so positive and so supportive of people and who gives so much time to helping people in the community. She simply wrote: "Good power word." And then she added this note: "I often wonder how each topic becomes the week's focus. Probably his will in sending us a message." (From Helen Shaw, one of the finest Christian ladies that God has ever created. She is a gem. There are treasures in heaven waiting for her that are greater than most of us will receive.)

Section two of this book is about how each topic becomes the week's focus. It really is quite random. People often ask, "What is the Power Word going to be tomorrow?" I simply respond, "I don't know. The Lord hasn't told me yet!" And I mean that quite sincerely. Most of the time, I don't have a clue what will be written on Monday morning. I believe God does this purposefully. He wants to control the word for the day. That requires that I consult with him so it doesn't become simply my thoughts or my musings that lack substance and power.

This section seeks to help everyone see that God is talking all the time in various ways throughout our daily lives, 24/7! He is not just talking to me but to everyone who lives with the deposit of his Spirit in their lives. Our life is one ongoing conversation with God in every moment and in every place we find ourselves if we are just listening and observing and tuning our spirit to his presence.

The Monday Power Word comes from everywhere. Each chapter highlights the main source for the Power Word that got created and sent. There certainly is crossover in the development of the message. My mind is always popping, it seems, as I look back over my journal. I highlighted something more specific in each chapter in the hope that everyone can see that these same avenues of God speaking are available to all if we are just aware.

Each chapter gives examples of Power Words that arose from the source. If you have been a regular recipient of the Monday Power Word, I hope that you enjoy reading some of my favorites again. For those of you who are reading them for the first time, may they serve to encourage you in your walk with the Lord.

# Chapter 8

# THOUGHTS AND PROMPTINGS OF THE SPIRIT

Christians are people who live moment by moment in the presence of God. In fact, God is as close as the Spirit of God who dwells in each one who belongs to Christ. And he is a person. Doesn't it make sense, then, that we could have an ongoing dialogue with God through his Spirit who dwells in us? Should we expect that we might receive some specific direction from him? But there is always the haunting question concerning how he gives that direction. How does a person know whether he or she really heard from God?

In a book entitled *Listening to the Voice of God,* the writers state: "While God speaks in many ways, he provides an internal spiritual organ known as the human spirit that, when properly cultivated, is dependable in hearing God speak."[6] Following that, they refer to D. Martin Lloyd-Jones who described a more mystical approach in this way:

> Then God sometimes answers directly in our spirit. The prophet said, "I will watch and see what

he will say in me." God speaks to me by speaking in me. He can so lay something upon the mind that we are certain of the answer. He can impress something upon our spirits in an unmistakable manner. We find ourselves unable to get away from an impression that is on our mind or heart; we try to rid ourselves of it, but back it comes. So does God answer at times?[7]

I call what these writers describe "the thoughts and promptings of the Spirit." These almost always come into play with regard to the other ways in which he speaks, as will be addressed in succeeding chapters. So we start here to lay a foundation for the rest of the book.

## How Does He Do It?

The Scripture testifies that the Holy Spirit speaks. We know that he speaks through Scripture. How did he speak for Scripture to be written? Did he dictate Scripture to those who wrote it? I don't know any commentator or theologian who believes this is how the Bible got written. But there are at least a couple of places in Acts where it is recorded that the Holy Spirit spoke. Luke records that "the Spirit told Philip, 'Go to that chariot and stay near it'" (Acts 8:29). And in another place, Luke tells us how the church at Antioch decided to send people out to the mission field. "While they were worshipping the Lord and fasting, the Holy Spirit said, 'Set apart for me Barnabas and Saul for the work to which I have called them'" (Acts 13:2). Clearly, the Holy Spirit was directing the affairs of the church. There was no movement apart from the leading of the Holy Spirit. If we took these two examples literally, we would have to say that this speaking was audible. However, that would not seem to be the case in most places throughout Acts where it is noted that the Holy Spirit was leading and speaking.

I am reminded of how the plans and intentions of Paul and his companions got rearranged by God on the second missionary journey. Here is the way Luke recorded it:

> Paul and his companions traveled throughout the region of Phrygia and Galatia, having been kept by the Holy Spirit from preaching the word in the province of Asia. When they came to the border of Mysia, they tried to enter Bithynia, but the Spirit of Jesus would not allow them to. So they passed by Mysia and went down to Troas. During the night Paul had a vision of a man of Macedonia standing and begging him, "Come over to Macedonia and help us." After Paul had seen the vision, we got ready at once to leave for Macedonia, concluding that God had called us to preach the gospel to them.
>
> Acts 16:6–10

It would be instructive to know specifically just how the Holy Spirit kept Paul and his companions from preaching in certain territories that they attempted to enter. Did the Holy Spirit place obstacles in the path? Did he use the provincial authorities to keep them out? Just how did they determine that the Holy Spirit was keeping them out? One very specific way that played into their decision to pursue a particular direction came through a vision. Should we assume that the author of this vision was the Holy Spirit? Personally, I conclude this to be the case based upon the dominant reference to the guidance of the Holy Spirit in this account. And it is worth noting that all of this should be seen in the context that Paul and his companions were actively pursuing ministry. They were not just sitting around waiting for something to happen.

There is an interesting and intriguing statement in Acts that provides some broad insight concerning the presence of the Holy Spirit in the decisions of the church. It occurs in the midst of some debate and discussion over whether or not Gentiles should be circumcised as a condition for being a part of the community of God. After debating, discussing, and recounting the events that took place when the gospel was presented to the Gentiles, the apostles and elders of the Jerusalem church, along with Paul and Barnabas, came to the conclusion that an appointed group of leaders should be sent to Antioch with a letter concerning the decisions of this meeting. But here is the interesting statement: "It seemed good to the *Holy Spirit* and to us not to burden you with anything beyond the following requirements" (Acts 15:28). In this decision, there is a clear consciousness and sense of the presence of the Holy Spirit being involved in this decision.

I don't hear the audible voice of God. I doubt that few, if any, do. But I have experienced strong promptings and thoughts that did not originate with me. I can't think of any other source for them but God.

## Personal Promptings

The thoughts and promptings of God that come to our mind and spirit are God's attention-getters. They usually involve something that God wants us to see, to think, or to do. We get thoughts, insights, or direction that did not originate from ourselves. And it is easy to assess how serious God is about them. They will be intense, clear, and lasting.

God has clearly directed me to visit, call, or pray for certain people. And if I do not move on it the first time, he brings them to mind over and over again until I get it done. When I finally follow through with the prompting, the reason becomes evident through the performance of the action. God doesn't ask us to inquire, to visit, or to call a person without something critical being at stake.

In tense situations, God gives discernment concerning the true dynamics of a situation. Sometimes he works hard for us to just keep our tongues in check. If we are listening, we are saved from many transgressions. Sometimes he gives just the right words to say, just as he promised his disciples. God is still talking. It is a matter of us listening.

As I look back over some sermons from the past, I can't believe that I wrote them. Some of them are really good! Those words could not possibly have come from me alone.

There is no question that some of the Monday

Power Words originated from promptings. Here is one that jumped out at me. There is no doubt that God was getting my attention. The subject involved the tongue. Usually, when we recall what the Bible says about the tongue, we think about the warnings that James gives in his letter. But this Power Word took a different path.

So, check it out! Solomon writes: "The tongue has the power of life and death, and those who love it will eat its fruit" (Proverbs 18:21). That's a rather startling statement that eludes the casual reader and catches many Christians off guard. I mean, for Christians, we are fairly well versed in the dangers of the tongue. How is it that it is something we should love?

In the workplace, in general encounters with people, among family and friends, the tongue is always in operation. There is no question about its power. I would dare to say that all of us know its destructive power, both as receivers and transmitters of the word. But let us not miss that there is the power of life in the tongue. Silence accomplishes nothing!

Wholesome words build up. There resides a power in every one of us to give words of life to the people around us. Let us train up our tongues with words filled with the good things of life. They contain power to change the people around us. Through perseverance in good speech, we will overcome useless, idle, lame chatter that only displays the emptiness of life people have. People need to hear us. Love your tongue. Know that it can make a difference!

The different twist in this Power Word was not my idea. God awakened me to this Scripture.

Sometimes God produces a Power Word out of an area of great resistance in our lives. He just keeps bringing us back to something in our relationship with him until he wins. This Power Word got written on a Monday morning in May.

Today, the Lord placed in my mind the word wait. I don't know exactly why, except maybe because he knows that it is a word that drives me crazy. Yet, I know from years of reading devotional materials and various translations of Scripture that it speaks to an important element in our relationship to God.

Just an example from Psalm 25:4, 5 may help to clarify what's involved here. The King James Version of the Bible uses the word "wait" to express our position before God. "Show me your ways, O Lord; Teach me your paths. Lead me in Your truth and teach me, for You are the God of my salvation; On You I wait all the day." In the NIV and NAS version, the last phrase is, "And my hope is in you all day long."

What is stressed here in our relationship to God? It is a foundational trust in God who has given us life, who leads us in his ways, who teaches us his truth, and asks us to place our hope—the results he wants to work—in his timing. To not give up. To not get ahead of him. To work and to look to him in the confidence that what he proposes and intends to do will happen. In short, to wait on him, to rest in him, to allow him to do his work!

I don't know about you, but I need that today. Today, God alone needs to be enough. He is where the answers and results of our life rest. Wait on him! It is a position of trust and confidence.

That Power Word clearly arose from much dialogue with God. The word "wait" expanded into a whole flow of thoughts reflecting some ongoing, wrestling with God.

This same kind of dialogue with God is taking place in you if you are listening.

## How Can One Be Sure?

While I would not be dogmatic and promote 100 percent assurance about the promptings one might be experiencing, there are a list of elements that work together to give some confidence. These may not be exhaustive, but they are my list at the present time. You are welcome to add to the list and send the additions to me.

1) An abiding, daily relationship to Jesus. It is beginning our day, every day, by checking in with him, trusting him, laying our thoughts and desires before him. He promises to make our paths straight.

2) Obedience. "Anyone who chooses to do the will of God will find out whether my teaching comes from God or whether I speak on my own" (John 7:17).

# Chaper 9

# JOURNALING

It was good to hear it spoken by someone else. It makes me confident that I am not crazy. She shared her confidence that she was hearing from God and that sometimes her mind is just popping with thoughts. I knew exactly what she was talking about. There are times that God floods my mind with thoughts and insights. It is like kernels of popcorn. It begins with one kernel that pops and then another. Soon the whole popper is popping. It is exciting and exhilarating. But how does one capture all of it?

Gordon MacDonald wrote a book entitled *Ordering Your Private World*. Back in the 80s, my home Bible study group used it as a basis for discussion. All of us were interested in growing in our relationship to God. It was new material for all of us. This book introduced me to the practical task of journaling, although I don't believe I picked up the practice until years later. Embedded in one of the chapters was a discussion of journaling as a way to listen to God. Note what MacDonald writes:

> I became impressed by the fact that many, many godly men and women down through the centuries had also kept journals, and I began to wonder if they had not put their fingers upon an aid to spiri-

tual growth. To satisfy my curiosity, I decided to experiment and began keeping one for myself.

At first it was difficult. I felt self-conscious. I was worried that I would lose the journal or that someone might peek inside to see what I'd said. But slowly the self-consciousness began to fade, and I found myself sharing in the journal more and more of the thought that flooded my inner spirit. Into the journal went words describing my feelings, my fear and sense of weakness, my hopes, and my discoveries about where Christ was leading me. When I felt empty or defeated, I talked about that too in the journal.

Slowly I began to realize that the journal was helping me come to grips with an enormous part of my inner person that I had never been fully honest about. No longer could fears and struggles remain inside without definition. They were surfaced and confronted. And I became aware, little by little, that God's Holy Spirit was directing many of the thoughts and insights as I wrote. On paper, the Lord and I were carrying on a personal communion. He was helping me, in the words of David, to "search my heart." He was prodding me to put words to my fears, shapes to my doubts. And when I was candid about it, then there would often come out of Scripture or from the meditations of my own heart, the reassurances, the rebukes, and the admonishments that I so badly needed. But this began to happen only when the journal was employed.[8]

Everything that MacDonald wrote is my own experience. I could not explain the process more clearly.

A recent journal entry personifying the journal stated, "You must become my friend." Journaling became a serious part of my daily activity about five years ago after going through the experience of a sabbatical. I became consistent in recording my thoughts and activities. I could see God directing my steps and helping me to understand my circumstances. Soon after beginning a ministry in New York, I slipped out of journaling my daily relationship with Christ. It was not a conscious decision. It just happened. Some challenging times for my wife and I finally brought me back. Once again, God is bringing to mind Scripture, placing in my path people and conversation, awakening my awareness to life truths, keeping me awake with dreams, creating thoughts in my mind, and more—all which get recorded in a daily journal. It is a way God uses to help me find my way. That is how a journal becomes a friend. The record of those ways God is speaking helps to make the path clear.

## Journaling Is Not New

MacDonald recognized that the giants of the faith kept journals. That inspired him to give it a try. It is noteworthy to see that the Bible refers to journaling. It is called "chronicling." We know about the events of the kings because of the chronicling that occurred in those days. For example, it is written concerning Jeroboam: "The other events of Jeroboam's reign, his wars and how he ruled, are written in the book of the annals (chronicles) of the kings of Israel" (1 Kings 14:19). Tracing some of these references through the Scripture, one finds the "chronicles of the kings of Israel," "the chronicles of the kings of Judah," "the chronicles of King David," "the chronicles of Samuel," and more. The nation of Israel had a book of chronicles. Concerning the family heads of the tribe of Levi, it is recorded in Nehemiah: "The family head among the descendants of Levi up to the time of Johanan son of Eliashib were recorded in the book of the annals" (Nehemiah 12:23).

These records were extremely important in all the nations. When Haman plotted to put to death Mordecai, who had adopted Esther, the king became restless in the night that this was being planned, not knowing of the plot. It is recorded in Esther: "That night the king could not sleep; so he ordered the book of the chronicles, the record of his reign, to be brought in and read to him. It was found recorded there that Mordecai had exposed Bigthana and Teresh, two of the king's officers who guarded the doorway, who had conspired to assassinate King Xerxes" (Esther 6:1, 2). After consulting his journals, the king decided to honor Mordecai. Needless to say, it put a crimp in Haman's plans. Careful records gave the king some guidance that saved Mordecai's life. The king was likely oblivious to the working of God in all of this. The chronicles of the king were more about him than about God.

One might say that the Scripture is the chronicles of God. It is the record of God's dealings with mankind. It is a chronicle about him: his nature, his attributes, his plans, his will, his wonders, his grace, his salvation, his ways with us. All of it is given that we might know him and have life! It is a chronicle that saves, gives confidence, and delivers us from the gallows of Satan's evil schemes.

## A Place for Our Dreams

David wrote, "On my bed I remember you; I think of you through the watches of the night" (Psalms 63:6). A quick overview of the Bible indicates that there can be a lot of activity at night. I wonder if David planned these times on his bed. Or did God awaken him in a dream, and he just couldn't get back to sleep? All of us dream, and most of us don't give much attention to them. If we gave them more thought, might we find God speaking in some of them?

Recalling once again the day of Pentecost, Peter quoted the prophet Joel, who wrote concerning the last days: "Your sons and daughters will prophesy, your young men will see visions, your old men will dream dreams" (Acts 2:17). Did he mean it, or were these just words that were written so that we could endlessly explain them away?

My daughter Janelle is a dreamer. Once in a while she will share one of her dreams. They are truly amazing and complicated. I inquired about her most recent dream, thinking that I might use it here. It was so long and complicated, consisting of strange people who didn't even know one another. All of us who listened were worn out by the time she finished. Her dreams would give Carl Jung months of investigation. Daniel might even be challenged by her dreams. But I wonder if God is talking to her. What might he be saying if it is him?

A study of dreams and dreamers in the Bible raises some caution about getting our direction from dreams. Jeremiah records some statements of dreamers that have a familiar ring to what we hear from some people in our day. He writes about God saying, "I have heard what the prophets say who prophesy lies in my name. They say, 'I had a dream! I had a dream!' How long will this continue in the hearts of these lying prophets, who prophesy the delusions of their own minds?" (Jeremiah 23:25, 26). Sorting out a word from God or the delusions of our own mind requires some careful discernment. Journaling your dreams—whatever their content—is a way to find God's guidance if he happens to be the one providing the dream.

## Keeping It Simple

MacDonald gives some guidance about journaling that is helpful. The key to this practice as well as any other discipline of the Christian life is to keep it simple. MacDonald suggests just buying a simple book with blank, lined pages and writing one page a day. That's exactly what I do. I may not even fill a page on some days.

The dictionary defines journaling as "a usually continuous historical accounting of events arranged in order of time without analysis." The key words here are "without analysis." It is recording our thoughts, the Scriptures we are reading or that God bring to

our minds, our encounters, our insights, our dreams—
everything in our awareness—without analysis. The
time to analyze comes later, maybe once a week, after
you have made seven entries. Looking back over those
records reveals where your life is going. Themes of
thought start becoming clearer in your mind.

I know that my journal provides a foundation for
nearly all of the Monday Power Words. So I share two
Power Words to conclude this chapter. One Power
Word directly resulted from the journal. The second
Power Word reflects a theme that developed over a
period of time in which God kept saying to me that
there are no formulas in one's relationship to him or
in the performance of ministry.

### *A Steelers Defeat*

There are just some days that start like this, and
there is nothing one can do to dismiss the feeling.
I have started with one of those days today. I am
disquieted, disturbed in spirit, and feeling a bit of
depression. I didn't sleep well. One might blame
the humiliating defeat of my favorite team, the
Steelers. But that's not it. It started earlier in the
day, even before worship. Everything seemed out
of sorts. The visions, hopes, and plans leading into
this time began to unravel at the seams.

So here are the thoughts recorded in my journal this morning. Let me warn you, these are not
greatly encouraging.

"I have some disturbances today. I come every

Sunday expecting a breakout only to experience a letdown. I come looking for joy and excitement in the people of God only to witness complacency. I hope for people on Long Island to know Jesus in a real way only to witness their slavery to religious traditions that border almost on paganism. I believe in a better world only to wake up and hear that North Korea has tested a nuclear bomb. It all seems so meaningless to me. I feel like Solomon and understand his thoughts in Ecclesiastes. And to top it off, the Steelers looked horrible!"

Well, that's just me at the start of the day. Is there any question that I need a huge dose of God's Spirit today?

I am sure you have had your sour days and bleak outlooks. David did also. He wrote, "Why my soul, are you downcast? Why so disturbed within me? Put your hope in God, for I will yet praise him, my Savior and my God" (Psalm 42:11). Wow! God is bigger than all of this. I think I am feeling better already.

Never let go of God. Days like this can pass in the night, be buried in the depths, be removed far from one's memory as the glory of his presence casts a dark shadow over such senseless ramblings. Thank you for letting me ramble. I hope that you find something in this encouraging.

### *What Does It Take to Believe?*

What does it take to believe? Last week, one of the major news stories covered the release of photos from the Pentagon showing still shots of the plane plunging into the Pentagon building on 9/11. There are people who believe that all of this was a conspiracy—that this really didn't happen, that some missile caused the destruction, or whatever else they have concluded. The news media ran the photos, explaining that here was the nose of the plane and here is the plane on impact. The same photos were published in the newspapers. I watched the footage over and over and studied the photos in the newspapers. Honestly, as hard as I tried, I couldn't see the plane! Maybe it is just me.

It made me think about how hard it is to believe something. It reminded me of a conversation that Jesus told between the rich man and Abraham in Hades. The rich man wanted to send someone back to warn his family about this place. He said, "If someone from the dead goes to them, they will repent." Here is the startling reply of Abraham: "They will not be convinced even if someone rises from the dead" (Luke 16: 30–31).

This makes one think how difficult it is for someone to believe anything! It tells me that there are no five steps to salvation nor does jumping through a prescribed set of hoops make someone a believer. We probably don't know all that it takes for someone to believe. There is some mystery in this whole thing of how one totally trusts in Jesus.

Maybe that is it, not just for Christianity, but for all of life. We make things so complicated. I couldn't see the plane in all the footage and in the picture that was published. That bothered me a little. Then

I thought, where are all these people who were on flight 77? Did the plane drop them off somewhere in the deep jungle of the Amazon? Did it happen to cross the Bermuda Triangle, never to be found again? The answer to those questions makes it simple enough for me to conclude that this plane slammed into the Pentagon. Sometimes we've just got to keep it simple!

The night that I completed writing this chapter, I had a dream. As hard as I tried, I could not go to sleep. It was four thirty in the morning. So I got up, went into my office, and began writing in my journal. Here is what is written:

It is 4:30 a.m. The Lord has me awake with vision in the night. I can't go back to sleep. Here is the vision.

I found myself on a college campus—not a Bible college. I was there to speak, although I don't know the subject. However, at the end of the lecture, I announced that we would have a prayer service that evening at a particular building on campus.

When the time drew near for that prayer meeting, I arrived at the sight early to greet what I had expected to be a few in number. Prayer services are not greatly attended. People regard that as wasted time. I entered the building to scout out the room we would use. I found the room already in use. Going back outside, there stood before me hundreds of students.

We moved the prayer meeting to a field with bleachers that could seat the crowd. Speaking to the crowd, I began to speak, expressing how overwhelmed I was. I never expected to see that many people. I asked the students the question: "Can the world be changed, or can God change the world through prayer?" Then I realized that the question needed to be: "Can God change our world through prayer?" The question needs to be closer to us. Then I gave some instructions about praying from the depths of our desires and concerns—to make it real. That is where the dream ended.

What does it mean? Is it a prediction of something in my future? It was as real as anything in my life. It may never happen as seen in the vision. But it tells me that one, young people are desperately wanting something real and spiritual, and two, I am blessed and encouraged in the vision, and three, prayer is bigger than our general application which is, much of the time, dry and rote.

I almost didn't get up, but I couldn't get it out of my mind—the things that I have written concerning the night watches and the advice to have a notepad beside the bed. Would this be the time I finally did something myself that I have encouraged others to do? I still don't have a notepad beside my bed. Maybe now it will get done. I won't need to get out of bed to write.

We are going to get away for a few days for some time with family in Altoona and friends in Pittsburgh. I think we are actually looking forward to it. I am taking the journal along. I expect that God will be talking to me.

I still carry great hopes that God will fill the building at East Northport. It needs to become a deep desire in prayer by everyone.

Lord, we are still waiting your full redemption from past mistakes. Please hurry!

How much weight should I place in this dream? How can I determine what God is speaking? It is just one dream that must be placed in the context of other people and circumstances. But it did get me awake and writing. There are some loose ends to the first conclusions that I wrote. I believe that I will wait and see what else develops. I suspect that this may be an important dream in my life. It may play out in some different way than in the described vision. I do think that God is attempting to say something about my life. Time and personal decisions to God's leading will determine what actually develops. Stay tuned!

May all your thoughts, dreams, encounters, reading, and life situations converge on a clear path to a deeper relationship to Christ. You may want to try writing them down to help you on your journey.

# Chapter 10

# SCRIPTURE

No word is more powerful than Scripture. Unfortunately, many Christians struggle to understand its message, to see its relevance, and to experience its living power working in their lives. While the general population possesses a Bible, most people remain ignorant of its contents. Some of my friends in the community freely admit that they have no idea where to begin. There are thousands of Bibles sitting on people's coffee tables collecting dust. Clearly, the Scripture cannot be powerful as a closed book.

Many contemporary churches feel the pressure to make the Bible relevant so that people can get their arms around it. In many places, we are surrounding the Scripture with all sorts of high-tech media in order to make the Word exciting and interesting. I am not opposed to using any illustrative technique to highlight a truth in Scripture. However, as an everyday source of power in one's life, that just won't work.

I have never felt the pressure to make the Bible relevant. I have always plainly stated that the Bible is relevant. It touches every issue of our lives: money, sex, marriage, work, children, happiness, values, morals, death, eternal life—the list goes on. And there is one who brings it to life and makes it exciting. He lives inside every person who belongs to Jesus. He is the Holy Spirit, who is timeless—always contemporary. He dwells in us for the very purpose that we might know God, grow in him, and live in the adventure of life.

How do we explain the fact that so many struggle with this most powerful Word? I struggle to explain this problem. Some of my personal friends are highly educated people with professional jobs. They read more technical material than I can understand, but they can't get their arms around the Bible. Many Christians know the same experience. I think that many people simply have a brain freeze. I picture people grasping the Bible with their hands, and all of a sudden, they tense up and cannot think. I am sure the devil has something to do with this circumstance. A primer in the basic contents of Scripture could get most people over this problem.

Christians who know the contents of their Bible encounter a different challenge to some fresh insights from God for their daily lives. Too many of us approach the Bible as a textbook that requires studious investigation. While it is important that we attend a regular Bible school class, sometimes the study goes beyond some reasonable common sense. We parse words and dissect phrases to the extent that we lose the big picture of what the writer is addressing. We don't do this with any other book that we read. Recently, my brother-in-law was describing the intense nature of his Bible school class. While he appreciated the noble intentions of the teacher to be careful with the Word, he remarked that after his teacher gets done with the passage, not even the apostle Paul knows what he has said! We tend to squeeze the life out of Scripture.

While it is important to be careful about discerning the message of God in a right manner—to "rightly divide the word of truth" and to understand carefully what God has said—there is many times a tangential message underlying the thrust of the passage that is personal for each of us. Klaus Issler, in his book *Wasting Time with God*, provides this example of how a passage can speak to a person in a way not directly intended by God:

> Pastor Jack Deere was about to rebuke an older women regarding her conversation with a younger woman when Isaiah 42:3 came to his mind, "A bruised reed he will not break, and a smoldering wick he will not snuff out." Although a prophecy about the coming of Jesus and his gentle character, this verse was used to turn Deere's heart from irritation at the woman to compassion for her. "All it would take was one rebuke from her pastor to break her and snuff her out … The Lord was telling me that this was not the day to rebuke her, that he would handle her correction in another way, at another time." Regardless of how central or peripheral the significance, the more Scripture we study and memorize—becoming familiar with the very tone and texture of God's Word—the more the Spirit can illuminate his Word for us.[9]

Without violating the primary message of Isaiah 42:3, Pastor Deere heard a fresh word from God that directed his present circumstance and probably prevented him from sinning. God was still speaking and saying something personal to his life.

With regard to the Monday Power Word that is distributed to people every Monday, it is important to note that is was never intended to be a Bible study. The message intends to put a spark in one's thinking that will encourage the person through the week. While the Monday Power Word has various sources for that spark, many times God brings to mind an interesting, intriguing, or challenging Scripture as the means to drive the message. Most of the power words driven by Scripture are similar in application to the example of Pastor Deere. While the Scripture itself may have a primary meaning in its own context, the Monday Power Words bring forth some additional truth applicable to the present moment. These Power Words arose either from my own wrestling and relationship with God or from listening to people and knowing the circumstances they might be encountering. God brings to my mind some simple Scriptures that speak to those matters. It amazes me that most times it was just the right Scripture for many people. The response from recipients confirms that God was speaking plainly.

Here are some favorite examples of Monday Power Word. Maybe some of them are speaking to you today!

### *Lazy Fears*

"The lazy man says, 'There is a lion outside! I shall be slain in the streets!'" (Proverbs 22:13). Reading through Proverbs, one finds all sorts of startling statements like this one that just stop us in our tracks and cause us to ponder, *Wow, what a strange thought.* But it makes us think, right?

What about this one? Solomon has a lot to say about laziness throughout the book of Proverbs (cf Proverbs 6:6–11). This one simply reflects the truth that a lazy person raises all kind of excuses for not getting busy and producing, even to the point of raising irrational claims of danger.

And I think about myself. Many times I have entertained excuses for not producing. A lot of times those excuses involved the fear of speaking to other people. How many times have we failed to produce simply because we have looked at other people as lions, just ready to pounce on us?

There is a remedy for this. First, it involves prayer. If you are fearful of extending yourself to others, ask God for help, for courage, for boldness. You might be amazed by how he longs to answer that prayer. Second, it involves confidence. Fear of what awaits us when we approach other people subsides when we are confident in what we possess. Nothing overcomes like inner confidence. Put prayer and a growing confidence in what you possess together. There is no stopping that freight train!

No excuses. Get busy!

## Daily Dependence

"Give us this day our daily bread" (Matthew 6:11). I wonder how meaningful this statement from the Lord's Prayer is for our modern day Christian. In the days of Jesus, before his day, and even in some places of the world today, the needs of many people are met on a one-day-at-a-time basis. Myriads of people do not have a storehouse of supplies to carry them over some rough days or weeks. Think about those people who got stranded in the RV recently in the mountains of Oregon. They had food supplies that could keep them alive for many more weeks until they could be found.

I wonder how we would really fare as Christians if we were required to daily depend on the Lord for each day's need. Yet it is a prayer repeated by Christians on a weekly basis without any thought to its real life situation.

But if we do stop long enough to consider that we don't really control life—that in the next moment something could erupt to shake up our whole well-planned life, maybe we can get closer to it being a meaningful part of our daily prayer. God wants our relationship to him to be that of dependence. Such is a relationship of trust for whatever the need or the circumstance that might come. In that close relationship to him, life can throw us all sorts of curves, but we can continue living knowing that we are kept in his care and love. So if something is disturbing your spirit today, stop and ask him to supply your daily bread. You are probably right where he wants you!

## *Weary Goodness*

"Do not grow weary in doing good" (Galatians 6:9). Many times, these words hit a nerve. Are you a person who wonders if there is any value in doing the right thing, giving the best one can give, working above the call of duty? Does it seem that all the effort falls away to nothing? Are you tired? I think that all of us have been there and we need this encouragement from Paul.

Here's the complete context of his words: "Do not be deceived; God cannot be mocked. A man reaps what he sows. The one who sows to please his sinful nature, from that nature will reap destruction; the one who sows to please the Spirit, from the Spirit will reap eternal life. Let us not become weary in doing good, for at the proper time we will reap a harvest if we do not give up" (Galatians 6:7–9).

There it is, an irrevocable law of life! It is written by God into all things. It promises a true harvest. All the effort may not seem to be producing results. It may seem like the harvest is far off. But God is at work and he controls the timing. Don't give up. Get going. Persevere through the weariness. Don't be deceived by the lack of fruit at the present time. Trust in the law of God and his faithfulness to the promise. He will produce!

## Slicing Through the Muck

"Do your best to present yourself to God as one approved, a worker who does not need to be ashamed and who correctly handles the word of truth" (2 Timothy 2:15). To Timothy and to us, Paul teaches that a follower of Christ must be diligent about handling God's Word correctly, or more exactly, cutting the word straight, without distortion or perversion.

How necessary it is that we carefully study God's Word! In view of the explosion of information in our time, the rewriting of history, the distrust of the media, liberal education, and the conspiracy buffs that populate our society, it is critical that we who love Jesus apply ourselves more carefully to the study of God's Word. It is a treasure chest of truth, wisdom, and insight relevant to all of life in any age.

The call to study demands more work than just reading one of the many popular Christian books that flood the bookstores. It also requires discernment. Paul also instructed Timothy: "Watch your life and doctrine closely. Persevere in them, because if you do, you will save both yourself and your hearers" (1 Timothy 4:16).

Only God's truth can slice through the mucky world of information today. The truth of Scriptures will stand the test of any age. Find a trusted group with whom to study and learn the principles of handling God's Word correctly. Such will keep one's head from spinning!

There is a power word from God residing in every person reading this book. God is still speaking to each one of us personally through Scripture with the desire to bless our lives and give direction. There is an avenue of direction available to all of us. "Blessed are those … who delight in the law of the Lord and meditate on his law day and night. They are like a tree planted by streams of water, which yields its fruit in season and whose leaf does not wither—whatever they do prospers" (Psalm 1:1–3). "Oh how I love your law! I mediate on it all day long. Your commands are always with me and make me wiser than my enemies. I have more insight than all my teachers, for I mediate on your statutes" (Psalm 119:97–99). These promises are not limited to a particular class of believers or people for that matter.

But it does require that we open our Bibles and read. However, we need to read our Bibles the same way as we do any other book. Put aside the tendency to be studious and just allow God to have some time to speak. As we read, God will raise our awareness to some part of the passage that we are reading. A phrase jumps out at us and gets our attention. It makes us stop and ponder its significance for our life. Sometimes it is necessary to write that insight down in our journal and move on. Soon, over a period of time, God has stored up in our minds Scripture and insights that have accumulated through this relaxed time of reading his Word. At critical moments of decision or disturbance in our lives, God brings particular Scriptures to the forefront of our thinking, and he speaks to us.

This circumstance can be likened to Jesus' statement to his disciples when he told them that they would be arrested. "But when they arrest you, do not worry about what to say or how to say it. At that time you will be given what to say, for it will not be you speaking, but the Spirit of your Father speaking through you" (Matthew 10:19, 20). Remember that Jesus told his disciples that the "Advocate, the Holy Spirit, whom the Father will send in my name, will teach you all things and will remind you of everything I have said to you" (John 14:26). Jesus can only bring to our remembrance Scriptures and insights that first got into our memory banks. The truth is, he does it!

Everyone who has the Spirit of Christ is on track for hearing from God personally through Scripture. Just simply do this: Open God's book, ask him to speak to you, begin reading, record in your journal what you hear him saying to you, and listen for his word as he lives in you through the circumstances of your life. You will be writing your own Power Words for all of us to learn with you! We want to hear what God is speaking through you.

# Chapter 11

# MEDITATION

I attempted to find another title for this chapter. It scares me to think that someone might read the table of contents and immediately decide that they would skip this chapter. Meditation doesn't sound too exciting. Then I looked at the titles of the chapters in the second half of this book and noticed that they don't sound too exciting either. So I decided to call it what it is!

Meditation is always listed as a part of the Christian disciplines. That adds another scary word to this chapter: discipline. I would be willing to gamble that 95 percent or more of Christians hardly ever engage consistently in Christian disciplines. For all the promise that authors give to plunge into these activities, most of us find ourselves on the outside just wondering.

There are plenty of good books on Christian disciplines. I believe that *Celebration of Discipline* by Richard Foster is a classic. I know that a great number of us ministers purchased this book when it first came out. Foster cleverly used the word "celebration" in the title. Maybe he also knew that these disciplines needed some pizzazz.

The opening paragraphs of the chapter on "The Discipline of Meditation" are engaging. Here is what Foster writes:

In contemporary society our Adversary majors in three things: noise, hurry, and crowds. If he can keep us engaged in "muchness and manyness," he will rest satisfied. Psychiatrist C. G. Jung once remarked, "Hurry is not of the Devil; it is the Devil."

If we hope to move beyond the superficialities of our culture—including our religious culture—we must be willing to go down into the recreating silences, into the inner world of contemplation. In their writings, all of the masters of meditation strive to awaken us to the fact that the universe is much larger than we know, that there are vast unexplored inner regions that are just as real as the physical world we know so well. They tell us of exciting possibilities for new life and freedom. They call us to the adventure, to be pioneers in this frontier of the Spirit. Though it may sound strange to modern ears, we should without shame enroll as apprentices in the school of contemplative prayer.[10]

The rest of the chapter describes the misconceptions we hold about meditation, preparation for meditation, first steps on how to meditate, and physical exercises to help center. The content of Foster's chapter provides valuable help to learn this discipline.

I think I enrolled as an apprentice some time way back. I must have dropped out of school. I don't know if I ever practiced any of the exercises. Nobody would list me among the masters of meditation.

But I want the promises to explore inner regions, the adventure, the pioneer spirit, the exciting possibilities, the recreating silences. I believe that I have tasted some of all of these. But when I reflect back on how some of that meditation occurred and how it became a Monday Power Word, my meditation didn't look anything like what one might imagine.

Allow me to share a Monday Power Word here that arose from some meditation:

### *Peeling Potatoes*

I thought about a lot of things while peeling potatoes this morning at 7:00. My first thought: How did I get stuck with this job? It was supposed to be a pretty simple meal tonight: ham, potatoes, and green beans in the Crock Pot. There was only one problem. My wife left for work and left me the work!

There's nothing like peeling potatoes to get one's mind drifting. I began thinking, *There must be a better way to get these peeled.* I thought about doing it my wife's way, which involves using a knife to slice off the skin. But then I thought, *That makes a bag of five pound potatoes into two and a half.* I'm not into wasting potatoes. Then I thought, *Surely the restaurants have a slick way of doing this.* If they do, that wasn't helping me now. Whoever peels potatoes at restaurants sure gets a lot of time to think about things.

So the word the Lord gave to me while muddling through this task was patience. There is no question that this job required patience. And you know, I began to realize that excellence usually accompanies patience. I thought about just slicing up those potatoes with the skin on them. But the only picture that stayed in my mind visualized all that skin floating throughout the Crock Pot at the end of the day. That would not be very appetizing nor does it produce anything good.

Patience produces the good result. In the parable of the sower, Jesus taught, "Still other seed fell on good soil. It came up and yielded a crop … the seed on good soil stand for those with a noble and good heart, who hear the word, retain it, and by persevering (patience) produce a crop" (Luke 8:8, 15). Whether in our personal lives or in the ministry of the church, patience is usually the key to fruitfulness. So hang in there and keep persevering!

Foster writes about our desire to hear the living voice of God and indicates that meditation is a pathway to hearing God speak. He notes that some people don't want to hear God and cites the example of the Israelites who told Moses to get the message from God and give it to them (Exodus 20:19). Foster writes:

That is why meditation is so threatening to us. It boldly calls us to enter into the living presence of God for ourselves. It tells us that God is speaking in the continuous present and wants to address us. Jesus and the New Testament writers make clear that this is not just for the religious professionals—the priests—but for everyone. All who acknowledge Jesus Christ as Lord are the universal priesthood of God and as such can enter the Holy of Holies and converse with the living God.[11]

I concur with Foster's conclusion. I believe that meditation is one of many ways we hear the voice of God. But it is foreign territory for most Christians. How do we get Christians to meditate? Do we need to enroll as apprentices in the school of meditation, or could there be something else involved?

## Some Biblical Insights

It occurred to me that the Bible references the idea of meditation. What a revelation! I realized that I might have a hard time defining meditation if someone pressed me for clarity. In the attempt to understand meditation, I stumbled on some insights for myself. It is interesting that we read the Bible many times without reflecting on the words that we read. We associate words, like meditation, with something already in the orbit of our learned perceptions without seeing some of the nuances. At least, that is my experience with this discipline of meditation. (By the way, the Bible never refers to meditation as a discipline!)

So here are just a few insights I gained that may be helpful to you, or maybe I have just been a little slow about all of this. I found that:

### *Meditation Takes Place Somewhere Other Than Places of Normal Activity.*

This insight caught my attention with a reference to Isaac. Genesis records: "Now Isaac had come from

Beer Lahai Roi, for he was living in the Negev. He went out *to the field* one evening to meditate" (Genesis 24:62, 63). It struck me as odd that Isaac went out to a field. I don't generally associate fields with meditating! I couldn't get out of my imagination tall corn stalks concealing Isaac from everything around him. How do you meditate among corn stalks?

But this was enough to get me to look more at places to meditate. We know that Jesus went off to "solitary places" (Mark 1:35). David speaks about his desire to go to "the house of the Lord" to meditate. He writes: "One thing I ask from the Lord, this only do I seek: that I may dwell in the house of the Lord all the days of my life, to gaze on the beauty of the Lord and to seek him in his temple" (Psalm 27:4). There is nothing abnormal about these places of meditation. Although, in today's church, one might not find too much meditation occurring in our energetic worship.

How about the bed as a place of meditation? The psalmist writes, "My eyes stay open through the watches of the night, that I may meditate on your promises" (Psalm 119:148). David says, "On my bed I remember you; I think of you through the watches of the night" (Psalm 63:6).

This was the end of my exploration of places. I quickly came to the conclusion that there is not one specific place that meditation can happen.

## Meditation Is Something That Happens In the Heart.

This may not seem so startling to you, but in the context of steps to meditating and physical exercises to center, this insight seems to be a little less intensive. A psalmist wrote, "I remembered my songs in the night. My heart meditated" (Psalm 77:6). I think about my heart accompanying me wherever I am every moment that I breathe. It is possible to meditate without centering.

There is no question that setting apart certain times to just reflect and think are advantageous. But Eastern mysticism has made an economy out of this need. People go to appointed places and pay a fee to a guru that leads them in some exercises to help them focus. The technical term is called centering. It sounds like a lot of work to me. It is good to separate ourselves from the hectic activities of our day and find a place that is quiet. But I find that it is more productive for me if I just relax and wait for God to speak in my heart. It doesn't require nearly as much discipline. If we have ears to hear, we will recognize meditation occurring in our hearts.

## Meditation Is Something That Happens 24/7.

This insight goes against the grain of our normal perception. We usually think about set times and places for meditation to happen. But the Scripture says, "Blessed are those ... who delight in the law of the Lord and meditate on his law day and night" (Psalm 1:1, 2).

# The Lighter Side of Meditation

I share these three brief insights just to take the edge off some of our associations with meditation and open the door to some other possibilities for meditation to happen. You could be peeling potatoes and meditating!

Meditation simply involves thinking contemplatively or reflectively. It is allowing time for thought, which can happen anytime throughout the day or night. The places for meditation are as numerous as the variety of people. It is any place that is outside your normal place of business. For instance, for Jesus, who was always among people, a solitary place was necessary. For some of us who work from home, a busy mall might be a place for contemplative thought. For some ministers who get away from their work and travel to seminars, smoking cigars around a table of fellowship might stir deep reflections! These reflections are thoughts of the heart that may stay there unless the Lord moves you to reveal them.

Anyplace can be a place of silence for me. I love to sit beside the water at Northport Harbor and just zone out. But I can do that at the mall or while driving or while sharing good times with friends. It really amounts to having a heart that is quiet and open to receive the still small voice of God. Meditation is not all that involved for me, and it doesn't need to be for you. It can start by just slowing down.

Here are a few of my favorite Power Words that came from meditation.

## *Fishing*

Sitting at the Northport Harbor one day, I noticed that many people choose to fish from the dock. It didn't really get my attention until I noticed one man go out to the end of the dock, prepare his fishing line, and then cast it into the water. Within one minute, he caught a fish! After he unhooked the fish from the line, he cast his line into the water again. Eureka! Lo and behold, another fish. That got me to thinking, always a dangerous thing for me to do.

I admit that I don't know much about fishing. That was never something my family did. The few times I have gone fishing prove that I don't know much about it. But it intrigues me, especially when I think about the fact that the first four disciples that Jesus called to follow him were fishermen. A lot of the metaphors throughout the Bible involve fishing. This makes me think that I should learn a little more about fishing before I do too much Bible study.

Not knowing much about fishing, I believe that two things must be true if nothing else. Number one, you can't catch many fish if there are no fish to be caught. You must go where the fish are! Number two, the fish must be hungry.

Every day at the harbor is not like the day that I described above when the gentleman was catching fish. There have been other days when people cast their line from the dock into the water and didn't catch any fish. I was on a boat once for six hours with forty other people on the Chesapeake Bay, and only two fish were caught! I am reminded that when Jesus issued his last call to Peter, Andrew, James, and John to follow him, it was a night in which they caught no fish (Luke 5:1–11)!

So what do we learn? One needs to keep moving and keep fishing. You can't stop dreaming your dreams or abandoning your goals because of some down days. For Christians who are praying and dreaming big hopes for their family, friends, neighbors, coworkers, and acquaintances with regard to their relationship to Jesus, stay close to Jesus. He knows where the fish are. He promises that those who abide in him will bear much fruit. So keep praying, serving, believing, expecting. Keep fishing!

### *Waves*

Sitting along the water at the park in Northport, the movement of the water caught my attention. It was a relatively calm day, and the water was still, except when a boat would either motor into the harbor or leave the harbor. That's when I began thinking about waves.

Waves don't just happen. Something else needs to occur for a wave to be formed. Waves require some other source of motion. Usually, in this part of the country, some breeze is blowing, and one can observe a choppy sea. But this was a calm day. The sea was still.

But there was the movement of boats. With the movement of boats, one could observe the movement of water—waves, ripples. Take your pick. Several thoughts occurred to me. Number one, not all the waves were the same. Different boats created a different kind of wave. It was interesting. Some of the smaller boats seemed to create the biggest stir. Number two, waves need multiple sources of motion to continue. If there is not a constant passing of boats, the sea will go back to being calm.

This reminds me of the wisdom of Solomon when he wrote: "Cast your bread upon the waters, for after many days you will find it again" (Ecclesiastes 11:1). He is telling us to make use of what we have. Get something going. Make some movement. Create some waves.

Waves happen when we make some movement. All of us are gifted to do something. We don't make the same kind of waves. But one thing is certain. If we do nothing, the sea will remain calm and nothing will happen. And we just can't make waves once. We must keep our boat moving. So get out there today and make waves!

### Rescue Ship 2

Thinking about the evacuation of people from Lebanon and loading them on military ships set my mind to reflecting about all sorts of strange stuff. I believe the church can be likened to these rescue ships. Anybody, without condition, is welcome aboard. And like these rescue ships in the Mediterranean Sea, the conditions are not always the best, and it is not always pretty.

I began thinking about these people loading onto the ship. For some strange reason, it occurred to me that it might be a smelly trip for ten to twelve hours. Think about it. People had to walk toward the loading area, dragging all of their luggage they could handle. It looked like it was hot and stuffy. I can only imagine these people being sweaty, and yes, smelly.

This made me ask my wife about showers on military ships and cruise ships. I never really thought about it before, but I began to wonder how 3,000 sailors on a military ship or 3,000 people on a cruise ship shower everyday! Where do they get the water? My wife said that they must get it from the sea. I'm guessing she is probably right. It intrigues me; how do they do that? Most people probably never think about the process of how a ship keeps them clean. They just turn on the shower, and wow, it works! Somebody out there probably knows how this all works.

Now you are thinking, what kind of Power Word is this? Well, it got me to thinking about baptism. That's the bath of rebirth. It is where we welcome aboard all the smelly, stressed, sin burdened people and provide a cleansing new start. How does it work? I don't know all the answers to that either. Our faith tells us that Jesus meets us there and does miraculous work in which we are born again.

I don't need to know all the mechanics. I only need to know him!

So Paul can write about all who have become Christians: "Do not be deceived: neither the sexually immoral nor idolaters nor adulterers nor male prostitutes nor practicing homosexuals nor thieves nor the greedy nor drunkards nor slanderers nor swindlers will inherit the kingdom of God. And that is what some of you were. But you were washed, you were sanctified, you were justified in the name of the Lord Jesus Christ and by the Spirit of our God" (1 Corinthians 6:9–11). Wow, given that list, is there any person outside of the power of Jesus to make new?

Maybe it is just my mind that operates in a strange way, but I really believe it is more a matter that God speaks to me and to us when we are quiet enough to listen. He is a God who thinks about a lot of interesting stuff. He constantly inspires me to reflect on things I wouldn't generally think about. He is probably doing this to you also.

# Chapter 12

# CREATION

When I look back over some of my Power Words, the most surprising source for writing is nature. Nobody would ever associate me with Francis of Assisi. Francis of Assisi was a Roman Catholic friar and the founder of the Order of Friars Minor, more commonly known as the Franciscans. He is known as the patron saint of animals, birds, the environment, and Italy, and it is customary for the Catholic churches to hold ceremonies honoring animals around his feast day of October 4.

Many of the stories that surround the life of Saint Francis deal with his love for animals. The most famous incident that illustrates the saint's humility towards nature is recounted in the *Fioretti* (*The Little Flowers,* a collection of legends and folklore that sprang up after the saint's death). It is said that one day while Francis was traveling with some companions, they happened upon a place in the road where birds filled the trees on either side. Francis told his companions, "Wait for me while I go to preach to my sisters, the birds." The birds surrounded him, drawn by the power of his voice, and not one of them flew away.

I don't think about birds much, and I am certain that they have no desire to flock around me. That's why it is startling that I wrote a Power Word about birds. Here is how it unfolded:

I've been thinking about birds a lot lately. Certain phrases come to mind like birdsong, this world's for the birds, birdbrain, Larry Bird. None of this is related or makes any sense, but those things come to mind.

I never think about birds. But I was recently sitting on the patio one Saturday afternoon, and the birds seemed to be all around. They were chirping loudly. I figured something was up. For some reason, I walked out into the yard, where the grass was deep because I hadn't mowed it, and there, nearly buried in the grass, was a baby bird. I figured this is what's up! I really didn't know what to do. The bird didn't appear injured. My first thought was, If I reach down and touch this thing, it will be a remake of the movie The Birds. So I went back to the patio, sat down and just watched what happened. Every once in a while another bird would swoop down to inspect. It would sort of peck at the baby. After a while, I went back into the house. When I came back a few hours later, the baby bird was no longer there. I thought, Thank God this case got resolved.

And I've been thinking, with all the thousands upon thousands of birds that surround us, why don't we see more birds lying on the ground? Really, my thought was more like, Why isn't the ground filled with carcasses of birds? What happens to them? One thinks that the ground would be littered with dead birds. What a pleasant Monday morning thought, right?

Now I can only think how great our God is, how vast his wisdom, how great his design! Did not Jesus say, "Are not two sparrows sold for a penny? Yet not one of them will fall to the ground outside your Father's care" (Matthew 10:29, NIV). God's always on the job, and he takes care of these things. Are we not worth more?

More bird thoughts later!

# 24/7 Talking

When we think about God's revelation and about the knowledge of God, our rational and academic minds give great attention to the special, specific words of God recorded in Scripture. We dismiss the works of his hands as a less reliable source of insight. Yet, there is a familiar Scripture that speaks otherwise.

> The heavens declare the glory of God; the skies proclaim the work of his hands. Day after day they pour forth speech; night after night they display knowledge. They have no speech, they use no words; no sound is heard from them. Yet their voice goes out into all the earth, their words to the ends of the world.
>
> Psalm 19:1–4

Interesting, isn't it? There are words without sound that go out through all the earth 24/7. There is knowledge that is always on display! I have always been intrigued with the fourth day of creation, mainly because I don't understand it completely. If you have not read it for a while, here is what is written:

> Let there be lights in the vault of the sky to separate the day from the night, and let them serve as signs to mark seasons and days and years, and let them be lights in the vault of the sky to give light on the earth. And it was so. God made two great lights—the greater light to govern the day and the lesser light to govern the night. He also made the stars. God set them in the vault of the sky to give light on the earth, to govern the day and the night, and to separate light from darkness. And God saw that it was good.
>
> Genesis 1:14–18

I look into the sky, and I don't get it. If I can find the big dipper, I rejoice. I mean, it's incredible and awesome and amazing. But there are others who look and find knowledge. Isn't that just what the magi from the east did, and they received the reward of seeing the baby Jesus?

Creation was meant to speak. "And the heavens proclaim his righteousness, for he is a God of justice" (Psalm 50:6). Paul was even more specific about God's revelation in creation and the knowledge it gives. To the Romans he wrote:

> The wrath of God is being revealed from heaven against all the godlessness and wickedness of human beings who suppress the truth by their wickedness, since what may be known about God is plain to them, because God has made it plain to

them. For since the creation of the world God's invisible qualities—his eternal power and divine nature—have been clearly seen, being understood from what has been made, so that people are without excuse.

Romans 1:18–20

We are surrounded with a constant message from God in every place and moment of our life. There is a lesson he is ready to give if we just have the eyes to see or the ears to hear. It may not be as deep as the magi experienced. Mine certainly are not. But creation is telling.

## Two Lessons

I find myself becoming a little more like Francis of Assisi. This is a shocking disruption to my cerebral disposition. Here are two more examples of how a Monday Power Word came to be by observing nature and letting it speak:

### *Amazing Sparrow*

There was a day last week when the wind was blowing between thirty and fifty miles per hour. As you looked out your window, you could see the trees bending under the force of the wind. It just happened as I glanced out for a moment; I saw a sparrow dart from the tree outside my window straight into the force of the wind! I don't think about these things too much, but obviously it got my attention. How incredible that a little bird could do that!

It made me recall a Scripture from Psalm 104:24: "How many are your works, Lord! In wisdom you made them all; the earth is full of your creatures."

And my first thought for Monday to get our engines started is: Be amazed! If we just slow down a little and allow God to speak to us through his many works, life will take on a new perspective.

That thought is good enough on its own, except I can't get out of my mind another picture of people attempting to walk straight into a wind blowing fifty miles per hour. It is more comical than anything. We see people bent over into the wind, holding onto their hats with umbrellas turned inside out. It is just a little reminder that we are not designed to be birds. How much smoother and enjoyable our lives become when we align ourselves with the way God wired us. I know that is a perplexing search for multitudes of people, including myself, but we just need to check in with him every day, listen for his voice, and follow where he leads us. "Bloom where you are planted." If we just engage what we are assigned to do today, and do it well, Jesus will lead us to what he has in mind for us when he created us!

Adam and Eve attempted to usurp their design and become God. It works a whole lot better if we just let God be God and live in peaceful fellowship with him.

## Trapped Bee

As I was sitting outside alone under the patio umbrella, a bee captured my attention. Now if there had been a few others from my family sitting there, it would have more than just captured my attention. There would have been a mass exodus until I had taken care of the crisis. How fortunate for this bee!

Lately, I seem to have become a naturalist. I've never given too much thought to birds and bees. Now I wish I would have paid more attention to National Geographic.

I have noticed this before but have never quite thought about it. This bee flew under the umbrella and kept hitting up against the top of the fabric. It did this over and over, obviously looking for some exit to the free air. I decided to time its activity. One could easily see that the bee was getting more and more frustrated. It traced nearly the whole surface of the umbrella, many times coming to the fringe where it could easily fly into open space. And when it would get that far, I almost wanted to yell and cheer and say go for it. You're almost free. And then it would fly back to the top. From the moment I began timing its frustrating activity to the time it finally flew out from under the umbrella, it was thirty-five minutes. (I know, you must be thinking, does this man ever work?).

It occurred to me how much that bee's circumstance mirrors the lives of myriads of people. We bump up against the same old stuff of life, many times hitting the same conditions and places that have never given freedom. We fail to recognize how close and how accessible freedom really is. Think about how open that space was for the bee beneath the umbrella! I began thinking, how dumb is that bee?

It reminded me of the Scripture written by Paul with a heavy heart for his own people, the Jews. How hard they worked, seeking a dynamic relationship to God, only to come up short over and over. He writes, "Do not say in your heart, 'Who will ascend into heaven?' (that is to bring Christ down) or 'Who will descend into the deep?' (that is to bring Christ up from the dead). But what does it say? 'The word is near you; it is in your mouth and in your heart'" (Romans 10:6–8). Why do we make it so hard? Why do we work so hard? The Lord is as close as the air one breathes. Allow his life to breathe into you today!

May the wonders of creation speak to your hearts and minds throughout all the day.

# Chapter 13

# NEWS

God is in the news. A great amount of the time, he is the news. When Jesus ministered in the towns and villages of Galilee, the gospel writers recorded, "News about him spread all over Syria … Large crowds from Galilee, the Decapolis, Jerusalem, Judea and the region across the Jordan followed him" (Matthew 4:24, 25). People were aware of the news about him, and Jesus was aware of the news. In fact, he decided not to go immediately to Jerusalem because he knew that the Jewish leaders were looking for a way to kill him (John 7:1). But the city was buzzing about him just the same. "Among the crowds there was widespread whispering about him" (John 7:12).

The story of Naaman, who was the commander of the army of the King of Aram, provides an interesting study about God in the news. God raised up Elisha to be a prophet in Israel. The news about Elisha's powerful works captured the attention of the nations around Israel.

Naaman was a valiant soldier, but he had leprosy. The army of Aram had taken captive a young girl from Israel who became a servant to Naaman's wife. When the young girl heard of Naaman's leprosy, she said to her mistress, "If only my master would see the prophet who is in Samaria! He would cure him of his leprosy" (2 Kings 5:3). So a letter was sent to the king of Israel asking that Naaman be received into the land so he could be cured. The king of Israel believed it was a trap. But the Scripture records, "When Elisha the man of God heard that the king of Israel had torn his robes, he sent him this message: 'Why have you torn your robes? Have the man come to me and he will know that there is a prophet in Israel" (2 Kings 5:8). God was working through the news to accomplish his purposes.

All of the events of Scripture are set in the context of history. Matthew tells us that Jesus was born in Bethlehem "during the time of King Herod" (Matthew 2:1). Luke specifies that Joseph and Mary began their journey to Bethlehem in the days when "Caesar Augustus issued a decree that a census should be taken of the entire Roman world. This was the first census that took place while Quirinius was governor of Syria" (Luke 2:1, 3). Luke tells us that the ministry of John the Baptist began "in the fifteenth year of the reign of Tiberius Caesar—when Pontius Pilate was governor of Judea" (Luke 3:1) and identifies additional people to lock John's ministry in time.

God is always at work in the circumstances of our life. In Paul's sermon at the Areopagus, he explained about God that "from one man he made all the nations, that they should inhabit the whole earth; and he marked out their appointed times in history and the boundaries of their land" (Acts 17:26). Concerning our relationship to the governing authorities, Paul taught us to "be subject to the governing authorities, for there is no authority except that which God has established" (Romans 13:1). God is aware and is working in all the news taking place around us. He is deeply involved in the affairs of our daily lives and in the unfolding history of our world. We live with confidence as Christians because of our knowledge of this truth.

I present these observations in order to cause us to pay more attention to the news. As Christians, we tend to avoid the news of the day. I hear Christians remarking that it is too depressing and deflating. There is nothing good in the news. I agree that it can be overwhelmingly discouraging most of the time, but in the midst of the news, God is speaking all the time, if we just have eyes to see and ears to hear.

The newspaper remains a good source for finding a broader spectrum of news beyond the headlines. The following examples of Monday Power Words demonstrate the variety of ways that God is speaking through the news.

# HEADLINES

## *Hate Crimes*

Mel Gibson is in trouble again. Or maybe I should simply say in the news. Last year, he found himself in hot water because of the movie *The Passion of Christ.* The Christian community rose to his defense and made his movie an overwhelming success. This time Mel is in the news because of driving under the influence. Well, that's not really the issue, is it? Hollywood and most others could bypass this careless act and write it off quickly. No, that's not really what has him in hot water. It is the anti-Semitic rant to the arresting officer that has colleagues calling for his censure. This makes for a very interesting study in a lot of ways.

I was instantly reminded of Isaiah who cried out, "Woe is me! I am ruined! For I am a man of unclean lips" (Isaiah 6:5). Throughout Scripture, it is interesting to note how our lips and tongue become associated with who we are. Maybe that is a subject for another Power Word. But that is not what intrigues me today.

What I find so fascinating relates to how our culture has stumbled onto a teaching of Jesus, of which it is unaware. I cannot date when it happened, but in recent times we have legislated something we call hate crimes. These are crimes of the heart, which makes them worse than some acts of lawlessness. It reminds us of the teaching of Jesus when he said, "You have heard that it was said to the people long ago, 'You shall not murder, and anyone who murders will be subject to judgment.' But I tell you that anyone who is angry with a brother or sister will be subject to judgment" (Matthew 5:21, 22). Mel is not in trouble because he has done any bad things to Jews. No, it is because of what maybe he thinks about the Jews. Our culture sees that as more serious!

And isn't that what Jesus taught—that the things of the heart are more serious! That's why we need him so much. The real issues of life spring from the heart. And Jesus knows more about that area than anyone else. And so we must pray always, "Create in me a pure heart, O God, and renew a steadfast spirit within me" (Psalm 51:10). You know what? Jesus can do it, and he will do it. Stay close to him today!

## *Rescue Ship 1*

Once again, the Middle East spirals to all out war between "Lebanon" and Israel. (I put Lebanon in quotes because the facts are more complicated). Now, the nations who have citizens living in Lebanon are seeking how to evacuate safely.

Our own news media has been reporting on the evacuation effort of the United States. And true to form, some of it gets confusing and irritating. Has the United States been too slow to respond? Do we really have a good plan for removing 25,000 people from the area? Are the people being rescued receiving good care? You get the idea. Most of the reports lean to the negative view, even though one segment reported that we are the envy of the other nations who are attempting to accomplish the same task!

The whole scene, with people boarding military supply ships that were not made for the convenience of people, caused me to ponder some random thoughts. Hearing some of the complaints of the people who were rescued got my mind started. "It took ten hours." "There was no food." "People had to stand." How inconvenient to be rescued! What did people think they were boarding, an ocean liner?

Jesus told the parable, "Once again, the kingdom of heaven is like a net that was let down into the lake and caught *all kinds of fish*" (Matthew 13:47). The rescue ship carried a wide variety of people without discriminating. Even the complainers were welcomed and rescued!

The church can be likened to the rescue ship. We take everyone without condition. And like the rescue ship, the conditions are not always the best, and it is not always pretty. But rescue ships are not designed for vacations. They deliver people to a destination out of harm's way.

Ultimately, there is no better ship than the church. For all of our imperfections and problems, the church of Jesus still accomplishes his purposes. And all are welcome aboard!

### The Blame Game

Recently, the news reported the breakup of Paul McCartney and his wife. They had been married for four years. All reports during that time indicated a good, solid marriage. But now it's over. All that is left involves dividing the millions of dollars between them.

The most interesting part of the report is the reason

for the breakup. According to the newspaper, Paul blamed the media for the fallout of the relationship. The media had given them, over the years, too much attention! How odd! The very instrument that breathes life and fame into these people we know—whose whole identity depends on the media—now gets the rap for the problems.

It is a tactic as old as the garden of Eden. Adam told God, "The woman you put here with me—she gave me some fruit from the tree, and I ate it" (Genesis 3:11). Well, at least Adam admitted he ate it, but he just couldn't help himself. He attempted to argue that it wasn't his fault.

God didn't buy it. What is wonderful about this fact is that God doesn't have to play this game. His infinite love and grace does not require him to dismiss the true reality of what occurred nor to sweep the disobedience under the rug. He holds Adam and each one of us accountable. He took care of this once for all by his death for our sins.

The game is over. There is no point or benefit in blaming one's flaws, mistakes, and failures on anybody but oneself. Why do it? Jesus' endless forgiveness awaits us each time we approach him without blame. What an incredible God he is! Live in freedom and confidence today knowing that this is our God, and he loves us unconditionally!

# HUMAN INTEREST

## *The Unhappiest Day*

I awoke this morning to the news that this is "the most unhappiest day of the year." Yes, really! I didn't know this before, but January 22 is said to be the most unhappiest day. I didn't get the full details. I think somebody in England thought this up. That news explains why I felt a little down the moment my eyes opened. And then, to give it a double whammy, it's Monday! Oh, woe is all of us.

Really, though, I didn't get up in a down mood. For me, one day is almost like another, except for Sunday, when there is the celebration of Jesus in worship. Now that's a great day!

But the news did make me think of a Scripture written by Paul. He was discussing how people elevate one day over another throughout the year. If you want to do that, fine. But he teaches that we should not demand that everyone think the same on this matter. "One person esteems one day above another; another esteems every day alike. Let each be fully convinced in his own mind" (Romans 14:5).

But a few verses later, he says this, which is key for me. "For none of us lives to himself, and no one dies to himself. For if we live, we live to the Lord; and if we die, we die to the Lord. Therefore whether we live or die, we are the Lord's" (Romans 14:7, 8).

Living every moment with the Lord makes every day wonderful! Make sure you check in with him today, and he will speak to you in every circumstance. He will keep your day fresh and exciting!

## *Citizenship*

A remarkable picture was displayed on TV a few days ago. Standing before a government official, with one hand raised and another hand holding the flag of the United States, stood several thousand people who are now American citizens. These people represented over fifty different countries. What a beautiful picture to see people from all walks of life, all ethnic groups, all colors, standing united together! Sort of a picture of heaven, isn't it?

All of them stood there proudly with big broad smiles. They spoke about opportunity, freedom, voting, a new life. One just got the sense that this moment for them is for real, that these new citizens will contribute greatly to our way of life, that they will vote every time, that their new life will not be taken for granted, ever! For them, it is a defining moment that will never lose its power. It is a new start, never to be unappreciated, never to speak harshly about, never to undermine.

I think about how different it is for those of us who have inherited our citizenship. Many of us just take it for granted. Our juices don't flow for this country as they flow in these new citizens. Truly, this is a remarkable country. And it is good to witness this ceremony. It raises our awareness of the wonderful life we truly possess.

As a Christian, this scene makes me jealous for the work of God in the lives of all people. For what America is in that picture, God desires for the whole world. How he longs for a gathering of people who appreciate the new life we possess in him, who contribute greatly to the glory of his way of life, who live with a glow and smile on their face, who never give up but always persevere regardless of the obstacles.

One must wonder why we strive so hard to create this picture in the people of God. Maybe it goes to the issue of having inherited our place in the kingdom. Maybe we take for granted something that we really don't possess in the first place. Something that should be the natural product of the indwelling Spirit in our life becomes hard work. God intended to make us a display of his splendor through the work of his Spirit in our life. All the preaching in the world cannot make that happen if his Spirit is not really in us.

Nicodemus learned that the kingdom of God is not something we inherit. Jesus said, "I tell you the truth, no one can see the kingdom of God unless he is born again" (John 3:3). This is the defining moment for all of us. All of us enter the kingdom in the same way without exception. When the kingdom becomes our desire like a treasure found in the field, then we will go after it with all our heart. Being born into it makes all the difference in the fruit that results in our life. We'll look like those legal immigrants, free and happy and steadfast! This is just some food for thought.

# JUST STUFF

## *Rubik's Cube*

The headline intrigued me: "Rubik's Cube Toys with Us." The news article highlighted the recent rise in sales of the Rubik's Cube, a toy that rose to popularity in the beginning years of the 80s. Today, it is once again surging to popularity along with a "renewed interest in back-to-basics toys." It was that line that caught me for the rest of the article. Adreienne Citrin, a spokeswoman for the Toy Industry Association, stated, "It provides balance. We see so many electronic and high-tech gadgets. This is a swing back to basics. It's something people can understand."

How applicable is this insight to spiritual truth! Isn't it time for people to get back to basics? Centuries ago, God urged us, through the prophet Jeremiah, "Stand in the ways and see, and ask for the old paths, where the good way is, and walk in it; Then you will find rest for your souls" (Jeremiah 6:16).

The word and teaching of the Lord in the Bible builds a foundation for living and brings balance to one's life. It's time to search diligently for the "old paths." Those paths are timeless and lead to eternity!

# Gardening

I can't believe that I actually stopped to read it. Generally, I pass through the living section of the Sunday paper just to pass time or to tell myself that I am expanding my knowledge. It would be dishonest to say that I usually read anything. So why did I stop at a huge calendar under the title "Gardening"? I can't explain it, especially since I have never been successful at planting gardens and actually harvesting a crop. Somebody told me that a tomato is a weed. Wow! I can't even grow them.

But there it was, a thirty-one-day road map to perfect gardening. And I began to read some of the instructions for each day. That's when I started to think about our lives and how all of us are presently doing something now in the hopes of achieving some personal visions for the future. Sometimes we get down on how far we have progressed. And then I thought about these insights from gardening.

First, we must start to do something. Nothing happens by sitting around and just hoping without starting something. One must scatter the seed in order to produce a crop. Second, gardening is hard work. It about wore me out thinking about all that one needs to do to produce a spectacular garden or flowerbed. But once we have started, we need to persevere if we know that what we are doing is true and built on right principles. Three, our dreams require daily attention. As stated on day ten of the calendar, "Weed. Just do it!" Four, depending on what you are building for the future, some dreams just take longer. Day two, "Plant asparagus, but be patient—don't expect a harvest till next year." No wonder one gets so little at restaurants.

For Christians, we have an edge if we just live aware and touch base daily. Jesus said, "The kingdom of God is as if a man should scatter seed on the ground, and should sleep by night and rise by day, and the seed should sprout and grow, he himself does not know how" (Mark 4:26). Behind all the staring, effort, daily attention, and patience is our Father who longs for the success of his children. Keep pursuing your hopes and dreams till the crop comes!

God is talking through the news media and the newspaper. Christians must fight the tendency to insulate ourselves from the world around us because the news tends to be negative. God is in the midst of people's lives, whether the news is good or bad. If we train our eyes to see and our ears to hear, we will recognize messages from God around us in the news.

There are numerous Christians who hardly ever turn the pages of a newspaper. But if you want to capture some messages from God, buy the paper and turn every page. He may just cause something to jump off the page that you never thought would be interesting. God will draw upon the reservoir of Scripture already stored in your mind and put the news and Scripture together. Now that's God talking!

# Chapter 14

# LIFE

Sometimes I wonder if Christians take in the life that is all around us. We have the tendency to focus so much on preparing people for eternity that we forget to live life now. Jesus said, "I came that they may have life, and have it to the full" (John 10:10). I often remind people of Paul's statement about the appearing of Christ. He explained that the appearing of Jesus "has destroyed death and brought life and immortality to light through the gospel" (2 Timothy 1:10). It is right to proclaim our enlightened understanding of death and immortality. However, it is just as significant to stress that we have even greater insight to life here and now! Jesus brought both eternal life and life now to light.

I also enjoy highlighting for Christians that life now is to be enjoyed. Concerning his teaching in the upper room, Jesus said, "I have told you this so that my joy may be in you and that your joy may be complete" (John 15:11). Another Scripture that speaks to me over and over is found in the midst of Paul's teaching about the dangers surrounding possessions. We hammer over and over the cautions made about getting rich. But in the midst of the warnings, we find an interesting phrase about enjoying life. Paul instructed Timothy, "Command those who are rich in this present world not to be arrogant nor to put their hope in wealth, which is so uncertain, but to put their hope in God, who richly provides us with everything for our enjoyment" (1 Timothy 6:17). Put in their proper perspective with respect to God, possessions are given to us for our enjoyment. That truth hardly ever gets headlines in the church.

Salvation is more than an insurance policy for life after death. Concerning our redemption, Peter states, "For you know that it was not with perishable things such as silver or gold that *you were redeemed from the empty way of life* handed down to you from your ancestor, but with the precious blood of Christ" (1 Peter 1:18, 19). Jesus rescues us now from a life that was going nowhere and places us in newness of life. Paul's prayer for us is that we might "be filled to the measure of all the fullness of God" (Ephesians 3:19). It appears that God had something more in mind when he saved us than just putting our life on hold until we died!

Our life consists of a dynamic relationship to Jesus, who is as close to us as we are to ourselves. "I have been crucified with Christ and I no longer live, but Christ lives in me" (Galatians 2:20). Should we not expect that in the affairs of our life, God might be speaking a message to inform our living? I believe that if we slow down and take in the life around us, we will hear God speaking to us constantly. God chooses to teach his truths through life experiences.

Much of our doctrinal understandings emerged from life situations. We see this over and over in the gospels. Jesus' most memorable teachings always followed some encounter with people in the midst of the normal activities of life. For example, the familiar statement of Jesus that "it is not the healthy who need a doctor, but the sick" and "I have not come to call the righteous, but sinners" arose from Jesus having dinner at Matthew's house, when the Pharisees challenged him about eating with sinners (Matthew 9:9–13). God speaks his most powerful messages in the middle of life situations.

The letters of Paul, which contain so much doctrine, are addressed to real life circumstances of the churches to which he wrote. That explains the reason for reading passages in context. Determining the true meaning of a passage requires that we crawl into the life situation of the original readers. For example, we might not have the very clear teaching about the resurrection of Christ found in 1 Corinthians 15, except that the Corinthian Christians had some peculiar challenges with the concept that Jesus rose from the dead bodily! We still have Christians who are challenged by that truth.

The truth that God revealed to us grew out of a present life context. It is not propositional truth, but life truth. The Bible is more a real-life story through which God teaches absolute truth about himself and about life. And he is still speaking truth through our own life experiences today.

I have learned to soak in more moments of life around me. In conversations with people, through observations of what people do, by enjoying the seasons of the year, God has made me see that he is still speaking in a fresh way. The following Monday Power Words illustrate how some life experiences became messages.

# PERSONAL EXPERIENCES

### *Young Again*

I feel young again. It's strange, truly strange. When I turned fifty, I figured that I was now on the slide. Walking through the malls and observing the mall walkers, I had already placed myself as one of them. That was a few years ago. Today, the energy is back and a vision of many more years filled with new experiences excites me.

Some of you may be wondering what happened! Simple. I became a grandfather on Friday night to a beautiful baby girl, Aubree Noel Hamer. All of a sudden, I feel invigorated, and I didn't even do anything. But seeing this new life has just thrilled my spirit. I am ready to invest a great deal of energy into her life. (Well, as much as I am allowed.)

All of it reminds me once again of the wonder of God. Reading through the final twenty-six chapters of Isaiah, one recognizes that one of the themes is God's challenge and ability to do new things. "Behold, the former things have come to pass, and new things I declare; Before they spring forth I tell you of them" (Isaiah 42:9). God is always into new things. He is never exhausted for ideas and for power to create. And those who are connected to him can always live the adventure of a life that is forever new.

Stay close to Jesus. He will always keep your heart young and your spirit fresh until the day you see him face to face. It is a life that is forever young!

### *That Was Close*

Close calls. That's what comes to mind today after this past weekend when my youngest daughter got married. Having planned and prepared everything well, we encountered some close calls that we never saw. I could make a list, but let me describe just one.

As the bridesmaids were lining up to enter the church, my daughter realized that she didn't have her blusher on. It is just her and me at this point, and I don't know what a blusher is, let alone how to put it on. I thought we were talking about makeup. So as we were standing at the door of the bridal room with the door partially opened, I waved to the bridal attendant to come over quickly. She took care of the blusher. We left the room to take our place for the entrance. My daughter then realized that she didn't have her flower bouquet. Oh no, now I'm frantic. The door to the bridal room was closed, and it is important to know that all day long, the door always locked itself when closed. Anyone wanting to enter the room had to knock to be let in. The music is playing, the bridesmaids are beginning to walk down the aisle, and I am frantically running to the bridal room, knowing that the door has not opened all day. Can you believe that the door opened? No kidding! No lying! And we got the flowers just in time.

I didn't think much about it then, but just after the ceremony, I couldn't help but think of the Scripture "Are not all angels ministering spirits sent to serve those who will inherit salvation?" (Hebrews 1:14). This may not seem to be some great crisis, but it would have been devastating for my daughter, after all that she imagined for her great day.

But it makes me wonder, how many close calls do we have throughout the day that we are not even aware exist? How great is our God! We must remain thankful for his care and protection for us. There are probably more close calls than we can imagine. But the Lord surrounds us with his angels, ministering spirits for life!

# Seasons of Life

## *Political Power*

The political season is in full bloom this week. What an exasperating way to live! It never ceases to end. And guess what? They have finally worn me out with all their ads, promises, and grandstanding. I know that the stakes are high, or at least we are told that. But when does anything meaningful ever get done by those who are our public servants?

I can't help but think about Pilate and how he attempted to maintain favor both with his political superiors and with the public in general. He didn't come off looking so courageous or powerful as he attempted to escape responsibility.

But you remember clearly the intriguing part of that encounter with Jesus in which Pilate said, "Do you not know that I have power to crucify you, and power to release you?" Jesus answered, "You could have no power at all against me unless it had been given you from above" (John 19:10, 11).

And there is what the political season is all about—power! You don't need to agree with me, but it seems, from my point of view, that this is the primary focus of most all of the ones running for office. It seems that they never stop running. No wonder we are tired.

But I take rest in the thought that ultimately all power rests in Jesus. And my life will not be drastically impacted by what occurs in the next week. For I believe that we who are Christians have in our grasp real power. This power is available for all. "He who believes in me, as the Scripture has said, out of his heart will flow rivers of living water. By this he spoke concerning the Spirit, whom those believing in him would receive" (John 7:38, 39). Stay focused on Jesus and seek him "and the things of earth will grow strangely dim" (Old Hymn: Turn Your Eyes Upon Jesus). I feel revived already!

## *Enjoying the Moment*

It's that time of year again. For most people—not all—it is truly the "most wonderful time of the year." But it can get confusing. My daughter shared that she hoped that the time would go slow, but she can't wait for Christmas day, and she doesn't like Christmas night. Yes, it was all one sentence, by a twenty-five-year-old! It speaks to the wide range of emotions we feel during this stretch of time from Thanksgiving to New Year's.

So this morning I thought about two Scriptures that might be useful to all of us to get the most enjoyment from the next thirty plus days. Paul wrote, "Be very careful, then how you live—not as unwise but as wise, making the most of every opportunity" (Ephesians 5:15, 16). Some older translations say, "making the most of your time." Same idea! Add to this what Solomon wrote: "However many years anyone may live, let them enjoy them all" (Ecclesiastes 11:8).

Both of these Scriptures advise us to enjoy every moment for what it is. It is good to plan for the future as a new year approaches. It is fun to look forward to those special days of the year when family and friends gather. But be patient and don't live those days completely until they get here. Make this moment count as one day that leads to the joy set before us not only at Christmas but all the days God has planned for us.

Living in a close relationship to Jesus leads to new adventures filled with purpose, excitement, and joy!

### Do You Hear, See, Know?

"Do you hear what I hear? Do you see what I see? Do you know what I know?" These are familiar words that ring out this time of year. They are really an invitation to all to hear, see, and know the wonder of God in a manger.

At East Northport Christian Church, we are gathering under the theme "Discover Christmas Again." It is true that through the centuries and under the assault of secularism, the core meaning of Christmas has become buried under layers of paganism, commercialism, consumerism, etc.

Some of what has happened to Christmas has been innocent. I think that in the attempt to improve the season, many thoughts and devices have been raised up to make it more exciting or glorious or wonderful. It is the pressure we feel throughout our lives to make the next celebration bigger and better than the previous. We get so far beyond the original that we start to lose the true reality of that which started the celebration in the first place.

Christmas doesn't need improvement—it just needs to be studied. God in a manger, set in a real time and real place with real kings and real people and real names supported by the reliable testimony of written documents that stand the test of any attack. Now that is marvelous, glorious, amazing, exciting, satisfying. Oh that people could only hear, see, and know what we know. Maybe we just need to ask them the questions that they might "Discover Christmas Again." Because we have heard and we can see and we do know!

# Daily Living

## *A-Game*

"I wasn't on my A-game yesterday." What a great statement! It inspired me to work harder. The statement came from a middle-aged man. The conversation began when I simply noted that it was a cold day to be working outside and that he was probably hoping for an early spring. This man had to work outside every day, all through the winter, servicing his customers. His statement referred to the day before, when he left work for a couple of hours to give blood. When he returned to work, he realized that giving blood took a little more out of him than what he expected. Thus, he wasn't on his "A-game."

You may be asking, "What makes this statement so inspiring?" Well, the significance arises from this man's occupation. This man simply worked as a gas station attendant pumping gas for his customers. And on this one day, he wasn't on his A-game. It was a statement that reflected the importance this man placed on his work. It was something that needed done well. He set high expectations for his performance. Yet all he does every day from six to six is pump gas. Don't you just love this guy for his standards of excellence?

It reminds me of that wonderful Scripture which states, "Go to the ant, you sluggard, consider its ways and be wise! It has no commander, no overseer or ruler, yet it stores it provisions in summer and gathers its food at harvest" (Proverbs 6:6–8). This gas station attendant is one of those antlike people that all of us can follow. He establishes high standards for his work. He seeks his A-game every day. I want to be in that company of people!

## The Starbucks Fellowship

Most days, I stop at Starbucks on the way to the church office. Usually it is about the same time in the morning that I get there. I finally noticed something that happens nearly every day at the same hour. Two tables are moved together, and around those tables sit six men, sometimes seven. Nothing odd about that except that it occurred to me how different was this gathering. Some men were old; some were young. One is well dressed; the others are either dressed for laborious work or for reclining on their couches when the meeting ends. Some are skinny; some are stout! Some have well-manicured hair; others either had no hair or just let their hair be whatever it is when getting out of bed. It just doesn't seem to be a group that fits.

That's pretty much like the church. God has brought together a group of people that don't quite fit. And what a beautiful sight! John wrote, "After this I looked, and there before me was a great multitude that no one could count, from every nation, tribe, people and language, standing before the throne and in front of the Lamb" (Revelation 7:9).

Can we see it—a mosaic of people arm in arm, conversing together, loving one another, lifting up the glory and wonder of God together? It is that to which we are called and for which we labor. Catch that vision with everyone who surrounds you this week.

## *Gracious Driving*

Having lived now on Long Island for a whole year, let me make note the gracious driving of people along Larkfield Road. Now wait, I'm serious. This is positive. It can be difficult to get into traffic on Larkfield from the side roads. But I have noticed that a great many people will let you in. (Not my daughter Janelle, though.) Many times cars will stop for no reason just to let another car from the side road get ahead. That's my experience. It's amazing! I wonder if some of these people realize that they are living the golden rule.

Even non-Christians refer to Jesus' teaching: "So in everything, do to others what you would have them do to you, for this sums up the Law and the Prophets" (Matthew 7:12). Now this may not be as easy as one might think. In all the religious and ethical writings down through the centuries, there is really no parallel to this statement. This is a new teaching and new view of life.

Some will say, "No, I have heard that many times." Yes, you have. But it usually gets stated in a negative form. "Don't do to others what you don't want them to do to you." Or to use the example of Confucius; he said, "Is not reciprocity such a word? What you do not want done to yourself, do not do to others." In its negative form, it serves as a basis of all ethical teaching. Just don't do to others what you don't want them to do to you. That doesn't always prevent them from doing bad things to you.

Jesus turned this around and made our outlook more proactive. It is not about just refraining from certain actions. What he advocates is a life of going out of our way to enrich the lives of others around us, to do our best to help people, to give someone a good word, or to let them in the line of traffic. It is changing the environment around us by proactively doing or saying things that people would not expect.

As you interact with the people around you today, ask Jesus to show you what you can say or do to positively impact the environment around you!

Can you see it? God is always talking in the midst of our lives, giving us fresh messages of his truth. It requires that we tune our ears to hear and adjust our eyes to see. It is living in the awareness that every part of our lives has meaning and purpose. What is God saying to you today?

# Chapter 15

# PEOPLE

"I got a word from God last night." There are hosts of people who dump that kind of statement on us from time to time. I referred to these people in the introduction. They make us a little uneasy about God talking to us in some personal way. As stated in the introduction, every communication from God must pass the test of Scripture. It seems that many of these people who get their direct guidance from God stray from explicit statements that God has made in Scripture. We should be cautious about whether or not they got a word from God or from some other source.

We can add the additional test of people to this statement. It would be helpful to ask the person, has this word from God been examined by fellow Christians with whom you fellowship? That can be a revealing question. Many times we will find that people who got a word from God are lone rangers for Christ. They are not committed to any particular church. They don't tend to appreciate any examination of what they received. Their word from God is meant to be accepted, not questioned! That is usually a good indication that it did not come from God.

Rarely, if ever, does God speak through an individual person outside the association with other people. Moses needed Aaron, Joshua needed Moses,

Peter needed Paul, and even the Lone Ranger needed Tonto! We were not created to live alone without God or without other people who live with God. God advises us to seek out the advice of other people to help in providing guidance and wisdom. "The way of fools seems right to them, but the wise listen to advice" (Proverbs 12:15).

When God speaks and wants movement on something, there is usually more than one person involved. Cornelius had a vision of an angel coming from God who was speaking to him. The next day, as the people from Cornelius were on their way to see Peter, Peter had a vision. When the visitors arrive at Peter's doorstep and find everything the way they were told, and when it is announced to Peter that there are visitors standing at his door, does anyone doubt that God was behind all of this? (Acts 10). God involved a number of people in getting his purposes accomplished.

God is still talking, and most likely to more people than just me! He is talking to me, and he is talking to you, and sometimes he brings us together to get his message delivered clearly. We should be listening to one another and paying attention to the people surrounding us at any given moment. There might be a message from God in that encounter!

Here are just a few places one might find God talking through various people.

## Books

Reading is a dangerous business. Not all books are equal in value. I warn Christians that just because a

Christian bookstore stocks a book does not necessarily mean it is a book that should be bought and read. Some discernment is required. Solomon warned ages ago: "The words of the wise are like goads, their collected sayings like firmly embedded nails—given by one shepherd. Be warned, my son, of anything in addition to them. Of making many books there is no end, and much study wearies the body" (Ecclesiastes 12:11, 12). Solomon thought that there were a lot of books in his time? I wonder what he would think about the plethora of books on the market today. It is enough to wear us out. And to think that I want to make my own contribution!

Having said this, books provide access to a broader range of Christian thought. Books offer a place for God to distribute his message to a wider audience. Paul knew the value of books. Remember that he wrote to Timothy, "When you come, bring the cloak that I left with Carpus at Troas, and my scrolls, especially the parchments" (2 Timothy 4:13). Paul evidently had a library for study. If we want to hear God, we need to read.

## Worship

Some people may make the assumption that people attend worship to hear from God. As a preacher for over thirty years, I am not as confident that such is the case for everybody. But all the elements for God to speak are present if we recognize the dynamic environment that is available. God promises to inhabit the praises of his people. There is prayer to invite God's presence, provision, and providence. The preacher is prepared to announce God's word. The worship leader takes us to the throne room of God. We testify that our blessings flow from God through the giving our of tithes and offerings. All together, it is a place God promises to meet us as we gather to seek him. Is it possible he might speak in clear and dramatic ways?

It was in a worship service that Paul and Barnabas received their clear marching orders to take the gospel to the Gentiles. "While they were worshiping the Lord and fasting, the Holy Spirit said, 'Set apart for me Barnabas and Saul for the work to which I have called them.' So after they had fasted and prayed, they placed their hands on them and sent them off" (Acts 13:2, 3). This account involves a whole congregation of people hearing from God!

## Church Counsels

Church business meetings are the last place most Christians would expect to hear God talking. Anybody who has ever been a part of the leadership of the church can tell numerous war stories from the multitude of meetings they attended. Most meetings begin with prayer, asking for God's presence and leadership. But it only takes about thirty seconds into the agenda before God is long forgotten.

However, like worship, the elements are present for the business meeting to be a dynamic encounter with God. First, it is the business of his church of which he is the head. Jesus has a great interest in the proceedings. Second, the people gathered in the room are the appointed leadership, called by the Holy Spirit to their position. These are people filled with the Holy Spirit. Third, every meeting begins with prayer. What a perfect environment for God to speak. At times, it does happen!

Luke records a business meeting of the church. A number of people in the leadership spoke. There was much discussion and debate. Ultimately, the leadership composed a letter for the Gentile believers in Antioch. It is noteworthy that Luke records this content of the letter: "It seemed good to the Holy Spirit and to us not to burden you with anything beyond the following requirements" (Acts 15:28). Here is a business meeting in which the Holy Spirit got in a word. It gives us hope that God can speak in the contentious business meetings of the church.

I share these three examples simply to raise our awareness that God speaks through other people. Nobody would necessarily find anything profound in this observation. At the same time, we may think more highly of ourselves than what we ought to think and casually dismiss the presence and the words of the people around us. Perceptive ears can hear God talking.

I close this chapter with two Power Words that arose from reading—one from a Christian source and the other from the *Reader's Digest*. Then I share a Power Word that got started from some prayer and God speaking over a number of weeks. It is a Power Word that got completed from the contribution of a friend. God had more to say that he needed to speak through someone else.

# Thinking

Charles Swindoll wrote, "Soaring never just happens. It is the result of strong mental effort—thinking clearly, courageously, confidently. No one ever oozed his way out of mediocrity like a lazy slug. Everyone I know who models a high level of excellence has won the battle of the mind and taken the right thought captive."

Do you want to rise above the level of mediocrity? Would you like to look back over your work-week feeling satisfied and fulfilled? Are you a person who aims higher? The number one requirement is thinking! That's a great challenge in our present culture. Just read and listen to the idle, coarse, and undocumented thoughts of people. So much reflects living that is below even the level of mediocrity.

But there is a prescription! "Finally, brothers and sisters, whatever is true, whatever is noble, whatever is right, whatever is pure, whatever is lovely, whatever is admirable—if anything is excellent and praiseworthy—think about such things" (Philippians 4:8). There is no mysterious path to soaring. Those who dedicate themselves to finding and thinking about the things that are excellent will soar every time. Make a commitment to thinking about the things that are excellent this week.

# Effective Management

"Know what you're going to do with the ball before you get it." A *Reader's Digest* article reminded me of this important phrase when playing baseball. It involves thinking through all the possible play options when the ball is hit to you. This is especially important in critical situations when the game is on the line. A man on third with nobody out in the bottom of the ninth with the game tied—now that is tense! If the ball is hit to you, are you prepared for the various options that will keep the runner from scoring?

It made me think about the Bible, our playbook for life. "For everything that was written in the past was written to teach us, so that through the endurance taught in the Scriptures and the encouragement they provide we might have hope" (Romans 15:4). The Bible addresses and teaches us about all the circumstances that life throws at us. Through daily meditation and study, we are able to see what confronts us and how to manage those circumstances effectively.

So, do you know what to do before life comes at you? Let's be faithful in studying the Word. He keeps us in the game!

# 7 *P*'s

Want a good foundation for successful living? Over a period of time, 7 *P*'s have come to my mind. Here they are: Praise, Presence, Provision, Providence, Promise, Power, and Protection. I can't say dogmatically that these are directly from God, but since March, I have just been adding *P*'s to my list as, somehow or from somewhere, they come to mind. Maybe there are more than 7 *P*'s, but seven is a good number, so try this on for size.

It all begins with praise. Praise brings us into the presence of God, who makes provision for our lives, whether we are good or evil, and who directs our lives in his providence, for he is always at work in the lives of everyone. There exist the sure promises of God to give us hope. And two great promises that surround every moment is the promise of his power and his protection, which keeps our lives steady and sure in every circumstance. Sounds like a good sermon series. Maybe someone should write it!

This is living like peas in a pod. That is a different kind of *P*, but it makes the point. Those who seek Jesus and welcome him into their lives find themselves just where God longs and desires for them to be. It can be heard in the longing of Jesus for Jerusalem when he said, "How often I have longed to gather your children together, as a hen gathers her chicks under her wings, and you were not willing" (Matthew 23:37). There is really only one question to be answered with regard to successful living. Are you willing?

# 3 More P's

Last week I shared 7 *P*'s for successful living: Praise, Presence, Provision, Providence, Promise, Power, and Protection. With the insight of a friend from Lancaster, Pennsylvania, you can add an additional 3 *P*'s: Penance, Prayer, and Peace. I love it! It makes for a complete sermon series some day. What a perfect complement to the previous seven.

Just follow it. Penance: "I acknowledge my sin to you and did not cover up my iniquity … and you forgave the guilt of my sin" (Psalm 32:5). Confession like that opens the gate to effective prayer. "Surely the arm of the Lord is not too short to save, nor his ear too dull to hear. But your iniquities have separated you from your God … so that he will not hear" (Isaiah 59:1, 2). To have our sins covered and to gain the ear of God can only result in peace, which is the full result of all *P*'s. Follow the *P*'s to life and productivity!

But the real Power Word today is partnership. I thank all of you for your response to this weekly e-mail. Look what happens when Christians think together and work together. "As iron sharpens iron, so one person sharpens another" (Proverbs 27:17). So stay engaged, both to Jesus and to one another.

That enriches one another's lives and builds his kingdom!

I can't think of a more fitting ending for this chapter than this last Power Word. We must be around people. Let's share what God is speaking to each of us!

# Chapter 16

# PRAYER

It happened this morning as I started my day and began to ponder this day's work. I was looking for some reason not to write anything today. I must constantly ask myself, *Why are you procrastinating finishing this book?* So much of what I think doesn't make any sense. So I gave more time to prayer, just to avoid, I suppose, needing to work! Then it happened. The Lord interrupted my eloquent discourse in prayer and spoke!

Here is how it all happened. As I was working in my journal, I decided that it might be a good idea to develop a prayer list. I had lost some discipline in praying specifically for people, concerns, family, friends, circumstances, and more. When I finished, it occurred to me that it was a long list. That was a little disturbing. Have I been missing something in my prayers?

I settled into the task, discipline, and call of prayer. I began addressing specific items on the list. Then it happened. The Lord just interrupted me in midsentence. My immediate thought was, *What are you doing?* I asked, "Are you not interested in what I am praying about? Am I boring you?" Then he spoke clearly: "Where is your category of outreach? What people do you have on your prayer list for salvation?" He hit me square between the eyes. I didn't have a category for outreach. What an embarrassment!

There is no question that all of us know that we should be praying for people who have not accepted Jesus. It is something taught straightforwardly in Scripture. There is no revelation necessary to know this truth as a part of prayer. But sometimes God just needs to talk to us about it. Needless to say, I put away this time of prayer and went right to the prayer list. I created the category of outreach and started listing the people for whom I want to pray that they come to know the Lord more deeply. How could I miss this?

The main point is this: God is still talking and many times he interrupts our time with him in prayer just to awaken our awareness of some things in our life that we may be missing, or he may just have other things to talk about. Prayer is a two-way conversation if we allow it!

This chapter serves as an example of God speaking through our conversation with him. When I planned the chapters of this book, I purposely decided that this chapter would be the last one. And I intended to write it last. Today, I really was attempting to avoid writing. God had something else in mind. So here it is, chapter 16, the last chapter, being written before some other chapters. God just does things like this!

## God Answers

How many of us actually expect God to talk to us or to answer us when we pray? Do we really believe that God hears and answers, or do we make ourselves believe? Do we expect to hear anything from him?

Jeremiah wrote about this invitation from God: "Call to me and I will answer you and tell you great and unsearchable things you do not know" (Jeremiah 33:3). Is this an invitation offered only to Jeremiah, or is there any possibility that we might claim it also? If it is an open invitation available to us also, it is an exciting verse to ponder. God invites us to call to him. He doesn't seem to be bothered with our interruption to speak to him. He states that he will answer. But he will more than answer the call. God goes beyond our call. He will tell us about unsearchable things. This statement harmonizes with the benediction that Paul pronounced to the Ephesian Christians: "Now to him who is able to do immeasurably more than all we ask or imagine, according to his power that is at work within us" (Ephesians 3:20). God does not run out of exciting things to do, and he is willing to share that adventure with us, his children. It appears that God has more that he wants us to see and know! We can't even imagine these things!

I believe that we are included in the invitation. David encouraged people to know this truth.

> May the Lord answer you when you are in distress; may the name of the God of Jacob protect you. May he send you help from the sanctuary and grant you support from Zion … May the Lord grant all your requests. Now this I know: The Lord gives victory to his anointed. He answers him from his heavenly sanctuary with the victorious power of his right hand. Some trust in chariots and some in horses, but we trust in the name of the Lord our God.
>
> Psalm 20:1, 2, 6, 7

David expected the Lord to take notice and grant the requests of the people. The answer of the Lord is what sets him apart from every other god. There is no greater example of this than the challenge of Elijah to the prophets of Baal on Mount Carmel: "You call on the name of your god, and I will call on the name of the Lord. The god who answers by fire—he is God" (1 Kings 18:24). This confrontation demonstrated to the people that the true God responds. After the prophets of Baal cried all day long, "Baal, answer us," Elijah simply spoke to God saying, "Answer me, Lord, answer me, so these people will know that you, Lord, are God, and that you are turning their hearts back again" (1 Kings 18:37). God answers to indicate his presence. It is a testimony of his readiness to respond.

The Scripture records numerous instances where God answered people. He answered regardless of the person's status. He didn't just respond to the mega-persons of the Bible. And it is interesting to note that he responded in various ways. Here is a short list of answers to prayer:

> Isaac prayed to the Lord on behalf of his wife, because she was childless. The Lord answered his prayer, and his wife Rebekah became pregnant.
>
> Genesis 25:21

> As the sound of the trumpet grew louder and louder, Moses spoke and the voice of God answered him.
>
> Exodus 19:19

Once again David inquired of the Lord, and the Lord answered him, "God down to Keilah, for I am going to give the Philistines forces."

1 Samuel 23:4

David built an altar to the Lord there and sacrificed burnt offerings and fellowship offerings. He called on the Lord, and the Lord answered him with fire from heaven on the altar of burnt offering.

1 Chronicles 21:26

I sought the Lord, and he answered me; he delivered me from all my fears. Those who look to him are radiant; their faces are never covered with shame. This poor man called, and the Lord heard him; he saved him out of all his troubles. The angel of the Lord encamps around those who fear him, and he delivers them.

Psalm 34:4–7

Moses and Aaron were among his priests, Samuel was among those who called on his name; they called on the Lord and he answered them. He spoke to them from the pillar of cloud; they kept his statutes and the decrees he gave them.

Psalm 99:6, 7

At Caesarea there was a man named Cornelius, a centurion in what was known as the Italian Regiment. He and all his family were devout and God-fearing; he gave generously to those in need and prayed to God regularly. One day at about three in the afternoon he had a vision. He distinctly saw an angel of God, who came to him and said, "Cornelius." Cornelius stared at him in fear, "What is it, Lord?" he said. The angel, "Your prayers and gifts to the poor have come up as a memorial offering before God."

Acts 10:1–4

Answers to prayer and to calling on the Lord indicated God's favor to the petition. The silence of God indicated the direct opposite. Through the prophet Isaiah, God addresses his surprise that the people of Israel expected to be heard by him.

Shout it aloud, do not hold back. Raise your voice like a trumpet. Declare to my people their rebellion and to the house of Jacob their sins. For day after day they seek me out; they seem eager to know my ways, as if they were a nation that does what is right and has not forsaken the commands of its God. They ask me for just decisions and seem eager for God to come near them. "Why have we fasted," they say, "and you have not seen it? Why have we humbled ourselves, and you have not noticed." Yet on the day of your fasting, you do as you please and exploit all your workers. Your fasting ends in quarreling and strife, and in striking each other with wicked fists. You cannot fast as you do today and expect your voice to be heard on high.

Isaiah 58:1–4

Micah also rebuked the leaders and prophets of Israel stating, "Then they will cry out to the Lord, but he will not answer them. At that time he will hide his face from them because of the evil they have done" (Micah 3:4). Saul, the first king of Israel who drifted away from God, had a difficult time getting God to answer. In regard to his battle with the Philistines, the Scripture records, "So Saul asked God, 'Shall I go down and pursue the Philistines? Will you give them into Israel's hand?' But God did not answer him that day" (1 Samuel 14:37). In another place, the Scripture states, "When Saul saw the Philistine army, he was afraid; terror filled his heart. He inquired of the Lord, but the Lord did not answer him by dreams or Urim or prophets" (1 Samuel 28:5, 6). The silence of the Lord is deafening in Saul's example.

Unanswered prayer is not the norm. It is not the place that God desires. What makes our god God is this active relationship through prayer in which he responds to the call of his people. God tirelessly works to keep this highway of prayer unobstructed. After pronouncing the woes of God upon the nation of Israel, Isaiah paints this vision of a renewed people:

> Yet the Lord longs to be gracious to you; therefore he will rise up to show you compassion. For the Lord is a God of justice. Blessed are all who wait for him! People of Zion, who live in Jerusalem, you will weep no more. How gracious he will be when you cry for help! As soon as he hears, he will answer you. Although the Lord gives you the bread of adversity and the water of affliction, your teach-

ers will be hidden no more; with your own eyes you will see them. Whether you turn to the right or to the left, your ears will hear a voice behind you, saying, "This is the way; walk in it."

Isaiah 30:18–21

God describes a day when this relationship is complete, to the point that "before they call I will answer; while they are still speaking I will hear" (Isaiah 65:24). This is the ultimate destination in our relationship to him! We begin that journey right here, right now, in unobstructed prayer by his invitation!

There are no Monday Power Words that do not arise from prayer. However, there are always some that are directly linked to the prayer time with God. These Power Words usually arise from times of distress or emptiness for something to write. Here are just a few that may be helpful to you.

## Determined Trust Regardless

My mind is thinking about all who are receiving this Power Word today. I know that all of us face decisions and possibly some crises that might arise unexpectedly. Some of us are encountering obstacles to our hopes, dreams, and actions for success. It can be enough, many times, to discourage us from exercising a determined trust in the Lord.

There is an oft-repeated Scripture that is very useful for times when we just want to throw in the towel. "Delight yourself in the Lord and he will give you the desires of your heart" (Psalm 37:4).

There is nothing wrong with the use of that Scripture except that maybe it gets overused. So it is important to read the whole psalm.

Psalm 37 calls upon us to exercise determined trust regardless of the circumstance, the job pressures, the uncompleted hopes and dreams and desires. We are strongly urged to quit looking at the success and benefits that others—people who don't care about God—seem to enjoy. That is a prescription for despair.

Instead, keep your eyes, your trust, your prayers on God who controls all things. Be at rest and "wait patiently for him." This is the place I need to be today and every day. But especially on those days when it appears that all hope is lost.

I need this today. Maybe you do also. If not today, store this psalm in your reading bank for those days when you begin to go down a path of not talking to him, and you must be called back!

May the Lord bless and make successful the work, the thoughts, the plans, the hopes, and the actions of all of you who receive this today.

## Rainy Days and Mondays

It was a line from a Carpenters song years ago that still sticks with people: "Rainy days and Mondays always get me down." Well, today it's Monday, and it's raining. What a combination!

This is one of those slow start Mondays for me. Maybe it's because it's Monday. Or maybe it's because it's raining. Or maybe it's because I'm out of routine for the start of my day. Or maybe it's because of certain irritants that just happen. Regardless of the reason or reasons, it's always good to have a foundation on which to live one's life and to maintain soundness.

Is this a slow start Monday for you? You know as well as I know, it happens. It always raises the question, how does one address this circumstance?

Two things come to mind quickly. Slow start days are good for reflection. Every day can't be lived in the fast lane. Slow start days become a reminder to slow down and meditate. Those who meditate on the law of the Lord are "like a tree planted by the rivers of water, that brings forth it fruit in its season … and whatever he does prospers" (Psalm 1:2, 3).

Two, while I have taken this Scripture out of context, the Hebrew writer encourages, "Therefore do not cast away your confidence, which has great reward. For you have need of endurance" (Hebrews 10:35, 36). There are days that disturb us or irritate us, or whatever. But we who know Jesus have an anchor for our life that gives us confidence however slow today may be!

Rainy days and Mondays don't get me down! They are good days to think and to recalibrate one's work and goals. Not a bad thing to do once in a while, after spending some time with God in prayer.

# The Day After

It's the day after, and it is always challenging to know what to do after a beautiful Easter weekend enjoying family and friends, dinner and talk, activity and walk. For some, maybe it was just a refreshing break, and it's not too difficult to get back into the groove. There will be other days. But the real challenge awaits those of us who experienced Easter on a higher level, celebrating the wonder and truth of the resurrection. Yesterday was more than just beautiful; it was exhilarating, exciting, life-changing. Jesus is alive, not just yesterday, but today, tomorrow, and the next day, every day! It's the day after, when we must come down from the spiritual high. What do we do?

It's hard to know exactly what the disciples did. After learning that the tomb was empty, a couple of disciples were on the road to Emmaus. Some were huddled in a room. The next week, they were still in a room. And some time later, we find Peter and others fishing. Sounds like a little slow start from such an unprecedented historical event.

Are you having a slow start today? Don't let it get the best of you. I think maybe the disciples experienced something of the same. But they eventually got their focus and changed the world by announcing the good news. My best advice: "Let us fix our eyes on Jesus, the author and perfecter of our faith" (Hebrews 12:2). There are more spiritual highs to come. For Christians, each day has its thrills living with Jesus!

The thrills and adventures in the Christian life are limitless. Let us take up the invitation of God through prayer and live in the promise of experiencing things in life that we cannot even imagine!

# EPILOGUE

Reflecting back on that Bible school class that invited people to discuss what it meant to have a personal relationship to Christ, Roxie's comments stood out for everyone. She was hesitant to say anything. Maybe she thought everyone would think she was a little wacky. Or maybe she thought it was her imagination. Or maybe she thought nobody would believe her. But she couldn't hold back any longer. Sheepishly, she said, "He also talks to us!" She shared that he sometimes talks to here through signs, through people who cross her path, through dreams, through stillness and through prayer. Everything she said confirmed so much for me in this book.

Interestingly, the air didn't suddenly go out of the room. Others shared ways in which they heard God talking to them. It seemed like a huge sigh of relief for everyone sitting there. A dynamic, personal relationship is more than a slogan for a great many people.

I don't think God stopped talking after the last word of Scripture was written. I believe he talks to me. I don't believe that he has limited that discussion to a chosen class of people. So I am interested in what God is saying to others. Sometimes it takes patience and painful listening to process what others are hearing. But in the end, it is worth the effort, if we can just get people to share.

Recently I added to the Monday Power Word the Power Word Extra. It consists of asking the recipients to respond to a challenging and intriguing Scripture and sharing their response with everyone else. I intended for this to become a means for everyone to be challenged, to seek God for insight, and to share what they have heard. We have only done four of these. The response has not been overwhelming. And given the responses that have been made, I think that I know the problem.

The Power Word Extra is not intended to be a Bible study. But the responses lean more to that aspect. We turn every Scripture into a study rather than just allowing it to speak to our spirit after bathing it in prayer. I surmise that most of the people probably think this is the intention of the Power Word Extra. Maybe they don't believe they are qualified to share. They don't know how to allow God to just speak to them in the inner voice of their spirit. More specific direction needs to be given.

While it is always important to study the Bible for clarity, the Power Word Extra seeks to solicit a response about what God is saying to you through the given Scripture. It means relaxing with God and with his word. Why do we get so uptight with Scripture? It is meant for our enjoyment and as a means of opening our ears to God.

God is still talking through a variety of means. I hope that everyone can just slow down, relax, and take a deep breath—both with God's word and life—and live in the presence of God who fills all of life with conversation. I think everyone will find that he is still talking to you personally and powerfully with insights that the rest of us want to know and to ponder. So let the conversation expand!

# ENDNOTES

*Chapter Two*

1   Jamieson, R., Fausset, Ar. R., & Brown, D., *A Commentary, Critical and Explanatory, on the Old and New Testaments* (Oak Harbor, WA: Logos Research Systems, Inc., 1997).

*Chapter Six*

2   Vance Havner, *Pepper 'n' Salt,* (Grand Rapids, Michigan: Baker Book House, 1966), 106.

3   Ibid, pp. 11.

4   Jim Cymbala, *Fresh Power* (Grand Rapids, Michigan: Zondervan Publishing House, 2001), 24.

5   Cymbala, quoting William Law, 25.

*Chapter Eight*

6   R., Barrier and D. L. Goetz, *Listening to the Voice of God* (Minneapolis, MN: Bethany House, 1998).

7   Ibid.

*Chapter Nine*

8    Gordon MacDonald, *Ordering Your Private World* (Nashville, TN: Oliver Nelson, 1984), 130–131.

*Chapter Ten*

9    Klaus Issler, *Wasting Time With God* (Downers Grove, Ill: InterVarsity Press, 2001), 167.

*Chapter Eleven*

10    Richard J. Foster, *Celebration of Discipline* (New York: Harper& Row Publishers, 1978), 13.

11    Ibid, 19.